KETT OF

CAMBRIDGE

an eminent Victorian and his family

by Anna de Salvo

NEC

NATIONAL
EXTENSION
COLLEGE

Acknowledgements

© National Extension College Trust Ltd.
First published 1993
ISBN: 1 85356 449 4

Thanks to Vic Franklin, Rattee & Kett
      Mike Petty, C R Jakes and staff at the Cambridgeshire Collection
      Peter Cowell, Mayor of Cambridge 1982–83, 1987–88, 1991–92
      George Swindles, Sergeant at Mace
      Janet Smith, Wymondham Archivist
      E F Mills, Keeper of the Archives, Jesus College
      Mary Wells
      Mrs E Kett
      Peter Kett
      Nora Rutherford
      Rosemary Haslop
      and colleagues at NEC

      for their help and encouragement.

Photographs: Chris Morton
Photographs courtesy of The Cambridgeshire Collection, Lion Yard, Cambridge;
Mary Wells

Printed by: NEC Print
Cover and text design: Squires Graphics
Editor: Claudia Pienaar
Project Manager: Judy Brass
Page layout: Mary Bishop

For Peter and Elizabeth Norman, with love

The National Extension College is an educational trust and a registered charity with a prestigious body of trustees. It is an independent, self-financing organisation. Since it was established in 1963, NEC has pioneered the development of flexible learning for adults. NEC is actively developing innovative materials and systems for distance learning options on over 100 courses, from basic skills and general education to degree and professional training.

For further details of NEC resources and supported courses, contact:
Customer Services
National Extension College Trust Ltd
18 Brooklands Avenue
Cambridge CB2 2HN
Tel. 0223 358295 Fax 0223 313586

Wymondham House

RATTEE AND KETT

150

1843-1993

ANNIVERSARY

"Caring for our past – building for the future"

FOREWORD

This book was originally planned as a few pages about the history of Wymondham House, for friends and colleagues at the National Extension College, an educational trust which has been based at the house since 1978. I originally found Wymondham House interesting because it still retains the atmosphere of a Victorian home, even though the rooms are now offices. Structurally, the house has been little altered, and externally it appears unchanged. Some of the original features remain, the heavy carved wooden doors, the narrow, steep back staircases, the fireplaces and the large entrance hall with its original floor tiles. It is not therefore difficult to imagine it as the family home of a hundred years ago.

Most intriguing though are the permanent reminders of the family who built the house. The initials GK appear in several places; on the stained glass window with the date 1883; carved on the stairs in two different places, and the house name is carved in stone on the house frontage. These things made me wonder – why choose the name 'Wymondham House' and who was GK?

The only information I discovered initially was from my colleagues who knew that the house was built by someone called Kett who was associated with the Cambridge builders Rattee and Kett. This therefore became the starting point of my detective work.

I met Vic Franklin, keeper of the archives of Rattee and Kett but the company was sold out of the Kett family in 1926. By coincidence, 1993, is the 150th anniversary of the founding of the building company, and the name Rattee and Kett is still well known in Cambridgeshire and beyond.

I then made my first visit of many to the Cambridgeshire Collection and made some exciting discoveries. Firstly, the house belonged to George Kett, son of the founder of Rattee and Kett and, according to Vic Franklin, "the person who really put the company on the map". Kett had also been a prominent and industrious member of Cambridge society, a local Magistrate and Mayor of Cambridge three times.

The local newspapers were an excellent source of information. Unlike their modern counterparts, reporters of that era reported on events and meetings verbatim, which made it possible to accurately understand the attitudes and issues of the times and gave a vivid insight into some of the heated discussions which took place within the council chambers.

After some months I had amassed a lot of information about George Kett's public life but little about his family life. Kett himself had researched and written a 'pedigree' of his family which began with the Ketts of Wymondham in the 12th century, and ended with his grandchildren but there now appeared to be no related Ketts remaining in Cambridge. It was strange that this branch of such a large family, who at one time were so numerous around the Hills Road and Station Road area of Cambridge, should have completely died out. I visited the family graves at Mill Road cemetery and found them sadly broken down.

In an attempt to pick up another thread I visited Wymondham village and their archivist Janet Smith. Janet was very helpful, providing lots of information about the Kett family and also, finally, news of a living Kett relative – Peter Kett. Peter kindly sent me some information which revealed that although Kett's eldest grandson (also George) had been widowed twice, he married a third time and his wife Edith had a child in 1949 – a girl, Mary Kett. That was the good news, the bad news was that Grandson George had died in Cambridge in 1970 and Peter had no idea where his widow and daughter were.

Armed with the year of Grandson George's death, I then went to the library to search through that year's copies of The Cambridge Evening News in the hope that I would find a death notice and an address. Without the exact date, however, it was impossible to know where to start and the librarian stacked up three huge volumes containing over 300 newspapers, for me to search through. Luck was very much on my side however as I found the death notice in the very first paper and it also gave an address .

On a very wet and windy Saturday I walked along Hills Road to Claremont to visit the house which had once been Grandson George's home. After explaining that I was researching the Kett family history the lady of the house was very helpful and said she knew someone who would be able to tell me the whereabouts of Mrs Kett and Mary. She also told me an interesting tale about Mrs Kett finding a second world war unexploded bomb in her back garden – but this, I thought, was another story!

Several telephone calls later I finally achieved what I had worked so hard for, a family contact – but what if they had no interest in their past family history? I need not have worried though. Having spoken to Mrs Kett on the telephone and then to her daughter Mary, now Mrs Wells, I visited Mrs Wells at her home in Gosport. I was overjoyed to find exactly what I had hoped – many family photographs, books and memorabilia, including pictures of Wymondham House when it was Kett's home.

The material lent to me by the Kett family has enabled me to complete the work, which has now become large enough to be called a book. Many times whilst working in Wymondham House on the book, I have imagined Kett sitting at his desk researching his family history, and somehow, I got the strange impression that he did not disapprove of my actions. I now hope that you also will enjoy this glimpse of the past.

Anna de Salvo works for the National Extension College in the Learner Support Department.

She left school at sixteen and worked for the Town Crier newspaper and the Cambridge Evening News, with a spell working at kennels and stables in between.

She studied for her 'A' level English Literature qualification through the National Extension College before joining the staff in 1991.

Anna lives in Earith with her partner Chris. They have six horses and ponies and a dog, Tessa.

CONTENTS

PREFACE

George Kett 1836–1914
Justice of the Peace and three times Mayor of Cambridge: 1891–92, 1898–99, 1901–02

PREFACE

On 7 December 1549, a Norfolk farmer named Robert Kett was put in chains and hanged from Norwich Castle. His body was left to rot for weeks after his death, 'left out for winter store', as the locals expressed it. On the same day Robert's brother, William, was hanged from Wymondham Church.

Robert Kett farmed at Wymondham, the Norfolk village home to the Kett family since the twelfth Century. By the sixteenth century, there was great unrest within the East Anglian community, caused by bad harvests and rising prices and aggravated by the enclosure of common land. In Wymondham the Kett and Flowerdew families had enclosed land for their own private use. A group of rebellious peasant farmers decided to combat the injustice, and they set about demolishing the Kett and Flowerdew enclosures.

There had been a long-standing feud between the Ketts and their neighbours, the Flowerdews, and upon arrival of the rebels, and in the hope of saving some of the destruction on their own property, the incensed Flowerdews suggested to them that they should create havoc at Kett's place. The gang obliged by leaving to attack the enclosures on Kett's land. Kett, instead of defending his property, listened to the rebels' complaints. Deciding that they were justified, he helped to tear away his own fences and then led his newly-organised band of rebels back to Flowerdew's, where he persuaded them to complete the destruction. Fired by this success, and joined by his brother William, Robert Kett marched his rebel group on towards the city of Norwich. Robert was not young, but a comparatively old man in his fifties. This makes his actions and his rejection of his own comfortable home more remarkable.

Kett collected many followers as he marched towards the city. Soon many hundreds of peasant farmers were under his command. Kett had initiated a petition against wealthy landowners to hand to King Edward VI, asking for better living and working conditions for common men against wealthy landowners.

For a while Kett and his men camped just outside Norwich, on Mousehold Heath. When holding meetings he stood on a makeshift platform under an oak tree. This famous tree still exists and is known as 'Kett's Oak'.

Marshalling his men Kett attacked and captured Norwich. However, this victory was short-lived. The authorities' attempts to negotiate with the rebels failed when the offer of a pardon for all but Robert Kett was rejected, so the Earl of Warwick's massive professional army was sent to recapture Norwich, overwhelming the peasant force. Robert Kett tried to escape but was caught at Swannington. He was held at the Tower of London for six weeks before being brought back to Norwich and executed. As he was dying, he had a good view of the market place, where 200 of his men had already been hanged .

Historians have suggested that Kett was only rebelling against local government, and that he had expected support from central government in London. If so, he must have been bitterly disappointed. For some years after the rebellion the Kett family, who had been wealthy landowners, struggled to survive.

Nine generations and nearly three hundred years later in June 1836 at Wymondham,

Norfolk, George Kett was born. Like Robert, George was to become a leader, although unlike his ancestor, George was destined to be an upholder of the law. He was to become so fascinated by his family history that he spent many hours, throughout his life, preparing a family 'pedigree' which traced his ancestors back to the sixteenth century rebels and beyond.

Although he revered his long-dead kinsmen, George was a true Victorian pillar of society, and his own family were all rather in awe of him. Apparently in his later years, when he issued an invitation to a family gathering, it was rather like receiving a Royal Command!

Wymondham House in Brooklands Avenue, now the offices of the National Extension College and previously George Kett's home, was the starting point for research into George Kett. His life, of interest in its own right, gives an interesting insight into Victorian Cambridge.

An abundance of George Ketts might seem initially confusing. To clarify:

George Kett 1809–1872 — With James Rattee the founder of Rattee & Kett, the Cambridge building company.

His son
George Kett JP 1836–1914 — The subject of this book, Justice of the Peace and three times Mayor of Cambridge.

His son
George Robert Kett OBE 1863–1933 — During World War I, George Robert organised and operated the National Service Scheme and was made Executive Officer for Food Control for Cambridge and district. Awarded the OBE for his services.

His son
George Kett 1891–1970 — Became Captain Kett, referred to in this book as 'grandson George'.

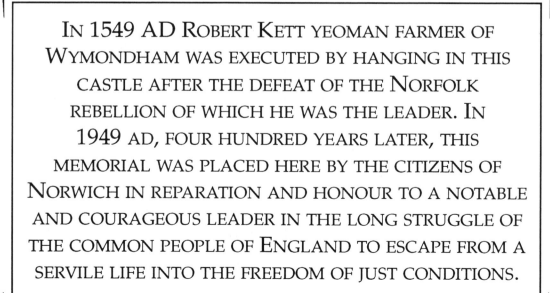

IN 1549 AD ROBERT KETT YEOMAN FARMER OF WYMONDHAM WAS EXECUTED BY HANGING IN THIS CASTLE AFTER THE DEFEAT OF THE NORFOLK REBELLION OF WHICH HE WAS THE LEADER. IN 1949 AD, FOUR HUNDRED YEARS LATER, THIS MEMORIAL WAS PLACED HERE BY THE CITIZENS OF NORWICH IN REPARATION AND HONOUR TO A NOTABLE AND COURAGEOUS LEADER IN THE LONG STRUGGLE OF THE COMMON PEOPLE OF ENGLAND TO ESCAPE FROM A SERVILE LIFE INTO THE FREEDOM OF JUST CONDITIONS.

Memorial to Robert Kett on the wall of Norwich Castle

ONE

BEGINNINGS

George Kett was born on 4 June 1836 in Wymondham, Norfolk, the village which had been home to generations of the Kett family since the twelfth century. His father, also George, was twenty-seven and had married Sarah Lincoln the previous year. He was a skilled carpenter and had established a small but successful business. The year after the birth of his son he was employed in restoration work at Norwich cathedral and the family moved to that city. A second child, Joanna, was born in 1838, and three brothers followed, Edmund in 1840 and twins William and Alfred in 1843.

While at Norwich, Kett senior met with James Rattee, a fellow Norfolk man. They established an acquaintance which was later to link the names Rattee and Kett. These names are still familiar to Cambridge people 150 years later.

One of the high points of George Kett senior's career was an appointment to work within the new Houses of Parliament at Westminster. His work pleased the architect Pugin[1] so much that he was employed for several years and was selected to carve the Royal Coat of Arms in the Chamber of the House of Lords.

The whole family moved to London during this period and young George attended a private school. Another sister, Susannah, was born in 1846.

Rattee & Kett, Station Road

---

1 Augustus Welby Northmore Pugin (1812–52)

James Rattee's beautiful house, pulled down in 1960

During these years, Rattee's reputation as a craftsman was growing. In Cambridge, Rattee had acquired the lease for a prime business site. Before 1845 this was a plot on the corner of a 'little lane leading to nowhere', but by 1848 the railway had been built and the lane became Station Road. James Rattee was looking for a partner. He arranged a meeting with Kett and the two joined forces to create the company Rattee and Kett, known initially as the Wood and Stone Carving Works, Cambridge. Kett was thirty-four and Rattee only twenty-three. Rattee's work, such as the carving of the choir stalls in Ely cathedral which was hailed by experts as, 'The most elaborate piece of art-workmanship executed since the reformation',[2] justified his suitability as a partner at such a young age.

The original works were built swiftly and were comprised of stone and joinery works, builder's yard and offices, with Rattee's house Poplar Cottage adjoining. The size of the workshops suggest potential for a substantial work force.

The Kett family together with their maternal grandmother moved to Petersfield, East Road, Cambridge, where the seventh and last child, Frederick James, was born in 1848. Young George left his school days behind and began work at his father's new business at the age of fourteen. He found the few years of private schooling he had received in London more than adequate for his business and later municipal success. 'Diligence', recorded the Cambridge Chronicle years later, was 'characteristic' of him and Norman Hillson of Downing College, Cambridge, paid tribute to George Kett in his youth. 'He began work at a very early age and astonished all who knew him by his energy and ability.' His father's company flourished, due to the combined efforts of the Ketts and James Rattee.

Rattee was a brilliant craftsman and an obsessive worker. He worked until exhausted, and on doctor's orders went to the continent during 1852, in order to restore his health. However, he seems to have spent his time there studying the principles of the master carvers in Lovain, Cologne, Hamburg and Antwerp.

He returned to work with enthusiasm, but his health was not good. In 1855, Rattee fell violently ill while at Guilden Morden, and was unable to fight an infection simply recorded as a 'cold'. Forty-eight hours later, he was dead.

2 'The Builder', April 21 1855

Rattee was buried at Cambridge Cemetery on the afternoon of Good Friday, where a large crowd gathered to 'evince their admiration of his abilities and respect for his character'. Both George Ketts (aged forty-five and eighteen) attended the funeral that day. Although Rattee left a widow who retained an interest in the business until her death, the responsibility for the running of the business now fell solely on Kett shoulders.

Hills Road, looking towards Regent Street

Hills Road, with Brooklands Avenue on the left

Pic of young George Kett

The original letter-head for business correspondence; later changed to 'Rattee and Kett'

TWO

MARRIAGE AND FAMILY

During the late 1850s young George went to London to organise some restoration work. While he was there he met and fell in love with Catherine August. Catherine's parents lived in Wicklewood, a village just a few miles away from Wymondham. The courtship was short and the couple were married at St Stephen the Martyr, Marylebone, London, in 1859. The bride was twenty-five, her husband twenty-four.

Catherine August was an only daughter. As Catherine Kett she had to adjust to being a member of a large family. Her six brothers- and sisters-in-law were all considerably her junior and, as the Kett children tended to live in close proximity even when they left their parents' home, she must have had to become used to the constant companionship of her husband's family.

Following a year of marriage Catherine presented her husband with a son, and the tradition of repeating Christian names through the generations was preserved when the child was christened George. However, unlike previous generations, George and Catherine's children were given two names, which helps with identification. This child, George Robert, used both Christian names throughout his life. He was, though, resentful

Brooklands Avenue, Cambridge

7

George and Sarah with their family
(George and Catherine stand at the right hand side of the back row)

of the two names – by family tradition eldest sons were given just the one Christian name, George. Displeased with this break, George Robert made sure that his own son was christened plain George.

The family returned to Cambridge during 1861 and settled at 15 Hills Road – which has now been renumbered 28. As the house is directly opposite St Paul's Church, the family had literally to cross the road to go to church on Sunday mornings. Later, Kett was to become Vicar's Warden at St Paul's. George's parents and their family moved to number 40 Hills Road (now destroyed), which was opposite Rattee and Kett on the Station Road corner.

George and Catherine's marriage was a successful one. Catherine was 'a true helpmate to her husband, whose charm and kindliness of manner have materially smoothed his path.'[3] Their six children were born within eight years – after George Robert (1861) came Edmund Joseph (1862), Catherine Sarah (1863), Alice Caroline (1865), Frederick William (1867) and finally Maud Mary (1868).

By 1871 the family had moved to Morley Lodge, Brooklands Avenue. The Avenue (as it was often called then) was a quiet place lined with trees and exclusive residences. When they were old enough, George Robert and Edmund set out daily on their short journey to the Perse Grammar school for boys on Hills Road.

Their grandfather also moved from Hills Road to a grander residence at 18 Station Road (the property of Jesus College), another exclusive residential area. Although the south side has now been destroyed, the remaining Victorian houses are an indication of prosperous households long since departed.

In 1872, at the age of sixty-three, old George died at home. He left behind a household comprising his widow (who survived him by thirteen years), and his two youngest children, Susannah Elizabeth and Frederick James (aged twenty-five and twenty-three at the time of their father's death). All four are now buried in the same grave at the Mill Road Cemetery.

George's younger brothers Edmund, William and Alfred were working in the family firm, and all except William continued to do so until retirement. It was George, though, who was eventually to become sole proprietor, and who looked forward to passing the business on to his sons, George Robert and Edmund.

Initially, George Robert had other ideas. On completing his education, he received his father's permission to enter medical school and went to London to train as a doctor in 1877. It was Kett's second son, Edmund, who showed a keen interest in the business; and

3 E Gaskell

George Kett I 1809–1872

his brother's wish to become a doctor might have been fulfilled but for unforeseen circumstances arising in 1881.

During the years following old George's death, business at Rattee and Kett had increased steadily. The company gained a reputation for excellence and in consequence won many contracts of work. In spite of the demands made on his time and resources by his work, George Kett entered local government in 1881 as a member of the Board of Guardians for the Parish of St Edward.

The children, 15 November 1873. Maud Mary (5) Alice Caroline (8) Frederick William (6), Edmund Joseph (11), George Robert (13), Catherine Sarah (10).

This created extra pressure, and he became ill and was unable to work. Edmund was at hand, but there was too much to do, and George Robert was summoned home to help. Although he may not have known it at the time, George Robert left his student days behind him forever. He was immediately sent to an important restoration job at Aldenham Church, and then was engaged for four years upon restoration work at the Roman Catholic Church in Norwich. He never returned to his medical training, for during this period, George Robert met and married Elizabeth Coles of London. Their first child was a girl born in 1885. She was named Catherine Elizabeth, after her grandmother and mother.

As soon as he recovered his health George was back at work. He was a frequent visitor to Norwich while the company's work on the Roman Catholic Church there was progressing. This letter, written to the Dean of Jesus College and dated 31 March 1884, is an example of Kett's activity during this period.

Reverend Sir

I found your letter on my return from Norwich Saturday evening and have looked through all my memos and papers connected with your works and can only find the enclosed estimates – Jones is not with them and I thought I had left his particulars with you, at any rate I had them at one time all together and I can't think where the rest now are. If you have not got them I am obliged to leave this morning by early train in connection with Mr Scott's trial. Will look into the matter again at once on my return to Cambridge. In the meantime hope you will excuse delay.

Your obedient servant

George Kett

The intriguing case of Mr Scott has now unfortunately faded into obscurity, and we shall never know whether the Dean had mislaid the papers or whether the fault was Kett's. Note the straightforward, honest style of his letter.

THE PEDIGREE OF KETT, OF WYMONDHAM AND CAMBRIDGE 1698–1913

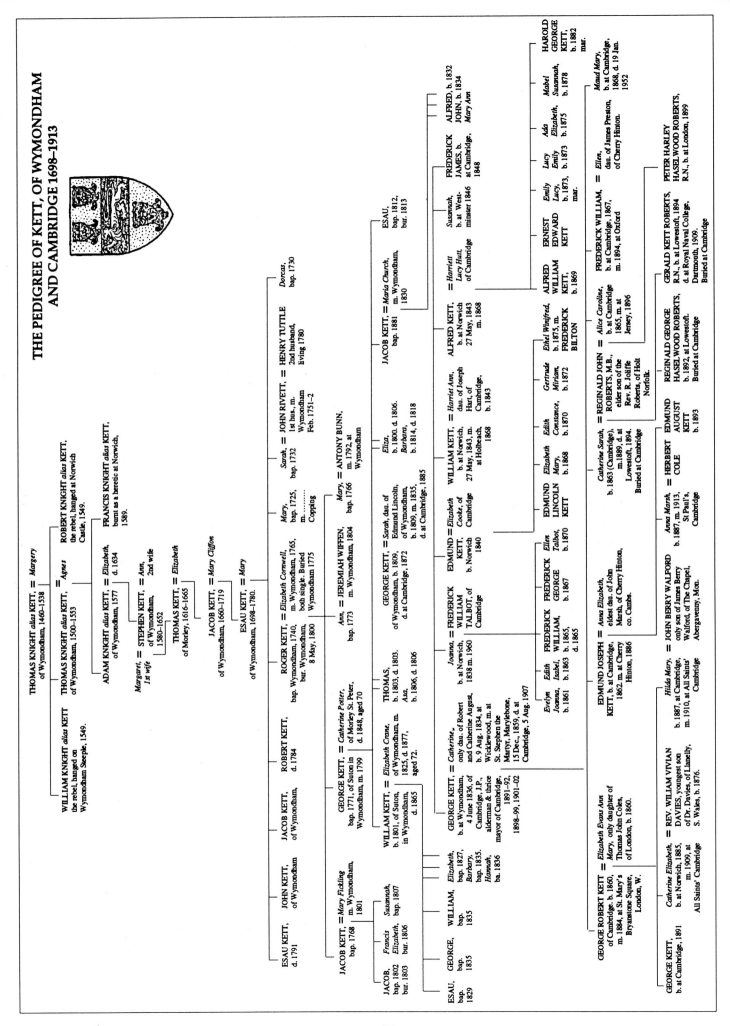

THREE

WYMONDHAM HOUSE

During the 1880s, the Kett family prospered, although George's mother died in 1885 in her 76th year. In 1879, Kett purchased a plot of land costing £880 in Brooklands Avenue, just a few hundred yards away from Morley Lodge. Three months later he purchased a second piece for £230, which adjoined the larger plot and a thin strip of land already in his possession. Wymondham House was built incorporating some of the same stone used for the Roman Catholic Church which was under construction in Cambridge at the time. The family settled in the house by 1883.

The house is an imposing building, in a Gothic style reminiscent of the Catholic Church. Some of the workmen building the church would have been employed to build the house. Features of the house include a stained glass windows with the initials G K and the date 1883 displayed, a beautifully carved staircase with the initials G K and also the initials of all six children carved around a central K. It is no surprise to find the house of the Master Carver elaborately decorated, with huge ornately carved fireplaces, doors and door surrounds.

The house was filled with good quality furniture. The bedrooms contained solid mahogany wardrobes and chests of drawers. In Catherine's room there was a folding writing desk which had belonged to her father – whom George always respectfully referred to as 'Mr August'. On the wall in the downstairs study was an oil painting of Queen Victoria, a walnut book case, a throne chair and a reading chair.

In the dining room a quality sideboard complimented the main table, while the drawing room contained a Chesterfield, several large upholstered easy chairs, and a statue by H Wiles, 'The Slaying of the Innocents'. Amongst other items were an oak cupboard, a brass and oak tray, a brass footman and two tall brass figures, indicating that someone in the family had a fondness for brass!

A Turkish carpet and hearth rug graced the drawing room floor. A Pembroke table resided in the bathroom, and a Grandfather clock marked time in the entrance hall. A piano and other instruments were kept in common with similar middle-class households of the time. There were plentiful quantities of household linen, plates, plated articles, china, glass, books, pictures, prints, photographs, silver – it was indeed a typically crowded Victorian home.

The children gradually left home with the exception of Maud Mary. She was an attractive girl who had inherited the family's artistic talents, a fine artist and a competent sculptress. But in keeping with Victorian tradition, one daughter was expected to remain at home to look after the parents in their old age. This was Maud Mary's role. She had once had a suitor, but her father had disapproved of him and there was no wedding. When Maud Mary finally left Wymondham House she was an ageing spinster of fifty-two.

The dining room

The rear of the house from the garden

The drawing room

George Kett just before his death

Wymondham House

Back Row (l to r): Alice Caroline, Edmund Joseph, Catherine Sarah
Seated (l to r): Maud Mary, George, Catherine, George Robert
Front: Frederick William

Maud Mary at work

Edmund married Anna Elizabeth Marsh of Cherry Hinton in 1886. Their first child, a girl like his brother's child, was born in 1887 and named Anna Marsh, though she was known amongst the family as Trixie. George Robert and Elizabeth had a second daughter, Hilda Mary, also born in 1887; but in 1891 they produced the long-awaited grandson, naturally named George. (Notice on the Kett pedigree on page 12 how George's place is before his two sisters, although they are older.) Edmund and Anna also had a son two years later, Edmund August, whilst the eldest daughter Catherine Sarah, who had been married in 1889 to Reginald Roberts, provided another grandson named Reginald George Roberts. Catherine and her family lived at Lowestoft, but the rest of the families lived near enough to be frequent visitors to their parents, who became Grandpappa and Grandmamma, after the fashion of the time.

FOUR

Proctors and politics

When the Market Ward seat on the Cambridge Town Council became vacant in March 1882, Kett stood for election. 'If elected, I will discharge the duties devolved upon me in such a manner as may be conducive to the welfare of the town in which we all have a common interest', he promised the voters. His candidature was successful, and the long association between George Kett and the Cambridge Corporation had begun.

Kett worked hard behind the scenes on the Council Committees, and little mention is made of him in the newspapers during this period. He was of special value to the Building and Finance Committees, and was promoted to the rank of Alderman in 1889, when he begins to be mentioned in the press. He was never guilty of making speeches for the reporters, as were some of his colleagues. He was also as conservative in temperament as he was in politics. Fellow Town Councillors and/or Aldermen during the 1890s were Horace Darwin, Mayor of Cambridge 1897 (son of Charles Darwin), Joshua Taylor, Mr Heffer, Mr Ginn and Mr Eden Lilley, all still familiar names to people living in Cambridge in the 1990s.

The Mayor's role a century ago was far more powerful than it is today. Although the Mayor's traditional costume has survived to this day, there are no longer Aldermen within the Council, so gone are the long red robes which they were privileged to wear on special occasions. However, Alderman Hill's gown has survived and is displayed in the Cambridge Folk Museum.

At the heart of both the Town Council and the community of Cambridge, two separate factors continued to be subjects of bitter controversy. The first was the ancient struggle between 'Town and Gown'. It was accepted that the University Proctors should rule over their students and police the University, but they also tried to extend their powers of jurisdiction over infuriated townsfolk. By tradition, Proctors were universally unpopular among the townspeople. The University was seen to be snobbish and the townspeople unruly. Centuries of trouble smouldered under the surface waiting for an opportunity to flare up – and it did so regularly.

The second source of discord was politics. New members of the middle class who had made their money through industry were generally Tories – and there was no stronger supporter of the Conservative cause than George Kett.

The Mayors of Cambridge during the 1880s had been predominantly Conservative, and this led to dissatisfaction amongst the Liberal Councillors. When the serving Mayor, Alderman Edward Bell died in March 1889, Conservative Alderman Wace was proposed to fill the vacancy. Wace's appointment was opposed by Councillors Nichols and Young, who suggested Councillor Bond for the Mayoralty. Nichols suggested that Wace, who was one of the new University Aldermen, could not be expected to serve the town before the University. Wace, after assuring the Council that there would be no such conflict of interest, was duly elected 17 votes to 9. Kett voted with the majority, who returned Wace to office again in November 1890. Certain members of the Town Council were determined to see a Liberal elected for municipal honours in 1891. Naturally, the Tories wanted to provide the Mayor from 'their side'; and the resultant conflict meant that the election of the Mayor of Cambridge for 1891 proved to be a very heated event.

There were two people set to suffer embarrassment by the strong political divide of the Corporation. Again the Liberal Councillors proposed William Bond, and this time the Conservatives chose George Kett to represent their interests.

William Bond

18

FIVE

MAYOR OF CAMBRIDGE

On 9 November 1891, the Guildhall was packed with Councillors, reporters and by-standers who had come to witness the election of the new Mayor. Alderman Joshua Taylor, a Conservative, rose and proposed Alderman Kett for the municipal honours. 'I am sure', said Taylor, 'that Alderman Kett will do his duty faithfully, fearlessly, and to the satisfaction of us all.' Kett's credentials were faultless. He was the 'head of a very large and prosperous local firm', a Magistrate, a hard working Alderman, and a family man.

Taylor's speech brought applause, but when the retiring Mayor asked for a member to second the nomination, the trouble began. An unidentified member, whom the Cambridge Chronicle and University Journal identifies as 'A voice', piped up 'The wrong grain'.[4] There was a long pause and no doubt a little shuffling.

After a while, the retiring Mayor was again obliged to ask for a second time whether anyone would second the nomination. Alderman Deck rose, and since political feeling was running high, could not resist the comment, 'I would have thought some member of the University, or some member of the 'other side' would have done so', at which cries of 'Oh! Oh!' arose from around the table. Deck praised Kett's abilities and said he had 'great pleasure' in seconding the nomination.

Liberal Councillor Campkin could keep quiet no longer. Agitated, he rose to propose another, 'who possesses all the qualities that have been mentioned by the proposer and seconder of Alderman Kett.' He proposed Councillor Bonds for the Liberal party, and his supporters applauded. Campkin attacked Kett in order to promote Bond's interests. Since the two men were as different as individuals could be, Campkin's comment that Bond did not 'aspire to the Mayoralty' indicated that he thought Kett did; and the fact the Bond was 'not in the same position' as Kett was another slight, indicating that Kett's advantages in terms of wealth and position were not fair. 'I might speak', insisted Campkin, 'for a great length of time upon the merits of Mr Bond', and proceeded to do so, encouraged as he was by applause and murmured 'hear hears' from his Liberal party allies. The Conservatives maintained a stony disapproving silence until Campkin concluded that, 'During the last twenty years, gentlemen have been proposed for the office of Chief Magistrate and elected without any regard for the claims of those who constitute a minority in the Council, but who are representatives of the majority of the town at large.' This could not be swallowed in silence. The Chronicle's columns report the indignant protests. Campkin carried on with his praise, and when he finally sat down his nomination was applauded, as Joshua Taylor's had been.

Councillor Nichols leapt up immediately to second Campkin's proposal – but his approach was different and he took some pains to show respect for Kett and handle the matter in a more diplomatic manner. 'I do not wish for one moment to depreciate the

---

4 Belonging to the 'wrong' political party.

value of Mr Kett's services', Nichols began, 'I do not think a more honourable man exists in the town, and I give credit for his business capacities. But he belongs to the party which dominates the Council, and which is determined at all times to monopolise not only the Mayoralty and the election of Aldermen, but every other situation which the Corporation has at its disposal.' Nichols appealed to the Tories, 'There is no gentleman on the "other side of the house" who can say that this is right.' He went on to suggest that Mayors should in future be elected alternately from one party then the other. The members laughed at this suggestion, but they were to remember it the following year. When Nichols sat down he enjoyed hearty applause.

The situation was unusual. Two candidates for the Mayoralty had been proposed and seconded. Spalding then asked to say a word or two. He was Chairman of the Conservative Party and Campkin would not let him speak, appealing to the Mayor that no-one had the right to speak on the propositions. Spalding however would not be silenced. 'Can I not propose someone else, then?', he asked, and permission was somewhat reluctantly granted.

Spalding got to his feet, and proposed the re-election of the retiring Mayor (Alderman Wace) and was responsible for creating a fleeting sense of unity within the Council – they all laughed at him! Spalding, undaunted, said that he thought it ungracious to oppose the election of Mr Alderman Kett, unless Mr Alderman Wace was re-elected. He then went on to sing Kett's praises, giving Campkin an ideal opportunity to interrupt. 'Mr Alderman Kett has been proposed and seconded.' Campkin turned to address the retiring Mayor. 'Mr Spalding should speak in regard to your qualifications, Sir!', which earned cries of 'Hear! Hear!' and the inevitable laughter. Undeterred, Spalding proceeded to praise Wace and propose him as Mayor. Councillor Flack asked if Wace would be prepared to stand if re-elected. 'I should certainly wish my friends *not* to vote for me', Wace replied.

Time was getting on and the meeting was not progressing. Councillor Dr Kenny got up to put in a word or two. 'By monopolising the Mayoralty as a prerequisite of one party, we shut off the possibility of calling to the Chair distinguished burgesses of the town who have not gone through the offices of the Council. For these reasons only', he explained, 'and not for a moment casting a slur on the character or qualifications of Alderman Kett, simply expressing a strong disapproval of an unfortunate custom which has prevailed in Cambridge for twenty years past, I will record a protest by voting for Mr Bond.' Councillor H Taylor quickly followed. 'I would like to see every Mayor of Cambridge discharge his duties with dignity, with fairness and to the satisfaction of all parties, not merely to the satisfaction of the representatives of the dominant party for the time being.' He took a breath. 'I will imitate my friend, Dr Kenny, by voting for Mr Bond.' This speech was hardly fair on Kett, but earned the speaker a smattering of applause.

Eventually, talking stopped and voting commenced. It was undoubtedly a tense time for both Kett and Bond, both of whom were the injured parties. Finally the votes were counted. The result: 27 for Kett, 17 for Bond. Kett could breath again, although Campkin and Nichols made for more unpleasantness by insisting that the voting be made public. (A list of who voted for who duly appeared in the Chronicle.) When the names had been read, Kett was declared Mayor, and invested with the Chain of office when he made the customary declaration.

It was now Kett's turn to speak. 'If I had the slightest idea that political options would run so high this morning, I would never have consented to be nominated to this office', he said. 'I think, and I earnestly believe, that every member of the Town Council is kindly disposed towards me.' Amidst a murmur of approval he continued, 'I never, for one moment, do anything which I think is in any way calculated to bring ill-feeling from any member of the Council. I feel no words that I could command would sufficiently express to you what my feelings are at this moment. It was mentioned that I aspired to the office of Mayor. I can assure you that it was something furthest from my thoughts. Situated as I am in business it is furthest to my wishes to accept office at the present time.'

After confirming his acceptance of the responsibilities of office, he went on to praise his opposition, Mr Bond. 'I am in favour of much that has been said by the proposer of Councillor Bond', said Kett, 'and I think it would have added considerably to the pleasure of taking office if it did not have that note of Party connected to it.' Kett finished with an assurance to the Liberal Party members that he 'respected their opinions as much as I do those who are in favour of the principles I hold.'[5]

Although his election had not been a comfortable one, good wishes and congratulations from friends and favourable reports in the newspapers helped to smooth the path as Kett began his first year of office. The employees at Ratte and Kett made a presentation to their employer upon his election as Mayor, which was the 'most welcome' of the good wishes and gifts that Kett and his family received following his election.

Catherine was unwell during 1891, and unable to take on the duties of Mayoress. The role was filled by 23-year-old Maud Mary, who remembered in later years the inconvenience of having to give up her 'afternoon nap', which she had been accustomed to all her life. The duties themselves she did not mind at all, but the illness of her mother cast a gloom over the household.

George Kett didn't have much time to be melancholy. He enjoyed personal good health and was used to a hectic lifestyle; as Justice of the Peace, as Alderman, as Director of his own company and others; as husband, father and brother.

Although Kett's social status was well-regarded in Cambridge society, he was still at heart a worker and businessman. His friendships were few but long-lasting, usually from the professional rather than the leisured classes, his greatest friend being John Morley, an architect who also served for a time on the Town Council.

As an employer, Kett had first-hand acquaintance with the working class, and treated his workers fairly. Although he paid higher than average wages for skilled craftsmen, he paid his apprentices poorly and all wages were decreased in winter. The workforce was reduced as and when necessary, but all these things were expected labour practice during the 1890s.

Kett believed that a worker should be paid a fair and appropriate wage, and fought for the increase of the Hall-Keeper of the municipal buildings salary from £40 p.a. to £175 p.a. in 1897. This was an increase of over 300 per cent, but it was justified by an increase in workload and included a sum to pay the salary of a full-time assistant. Although £40 p.a. had been considered by some as grossly inadequate, other Councillors strongly objected to such a rise, but Kett was adamant. 'On considering the extra duties devolving upon the Hall-Keeper, I am satisfied that the sum proposed is a reasonable and proper one.'

As Justice of the Peace, Kett dealt with petty crimes, and reproduced on the following pages are newspaper reports of some of the cases he judged during his years as a magistrate and the sentences he passed.

---

5 The following year, a Liberal Party member was elected as Mayor – Councillor Young – and Bond was promoted to the rank of Alderman. Again, the promotion of Bond was not without controversy. Two Councillors tied for the vacant Alderman seat, and the new Mayor used his casting vote in Bond's favour. The Chronicle sulkily reported that as three Conservative Councillors were absent at the meeting, the seat should have remained Conservative. The Cambridge Daily News thought that 'Tardy justice has been done to a man who has deserved well in the hands of his fellows.'

These Cambridge workmen were employed by Rattee and Kett in the building of Cambridge's Catholic Church in the 1890s – their wooden scaffolding can be seen in the church's interior.

COURT CASES

TUESDAY

(Before the Mayor (G. Kett, Esq.) and J. Barford, Esq.)

DISGRACEFUL CONDUCT

Augustus Barlow, of Jordan's Yard, Bridge Street, was charged with breaking the glass in a public gas lamp in Jesus Lane, the property of the Cambridge Gas Company, on December 24.

Defendant pleaded not guilty.

P.-s. Lilley said on the day in question, about 11.55 p.m. he was in Jesus Lane. He saw defendant, who was proceeding towards Bridge Street. When defendant reached the Clergy Training School witness saw him stoop down, pick up a handful of snow and make a snowball, which he threw at the gas lamp. The result was that one pane of glass was broken. Witness told defendant that he should take him into custody.

The MAYOR: How near were you to him at that time?

Witness: About ten yards sir.

The Clerk: What was his condition?

Witness: He had had drink, but was not drunk.

Defendant was further charged with using bad language in King Street and St. Andrew's street on the same day.

P.-s. Lilley said when defendant was taken into custody, he at once threw himself on the ground. P.-c. Clark came along and lifted defendant up. They then proceeded along Malcolm Street into King Street where the defendant shouted "Who the —— are you?" twice. He again threw himself down. They lifted him up, and went on by way of Hobson Street into St. Andrew's Street. Here defendant shouted "Who are you, you ——." P.-c. Clark gave similar evidence.

Charles Buttress, an employee of the Gas Company, said damage to the extent of 1s., was done to the lamp.

The MAYOR: What is the occupation of this man?

P.-s. Lilley: I have known him for some time and have never known him to do any work. He is generally about the street corners of an evening.

The MAYOR said defendant's record in the past had always been that of disgraceful conduct.

He would be fined 8s. for wilful damage and 2s. for the bad language. With 12s. 6d. costs. The alternative was 14 days' imprisonment.

ALLEGED THEFT OF MONEY

Fanny Elizabeth Laxton, of Compasses Passage was charged on remand with stealing from the person of Ernest Bendall, three sovereigns, on Dec. 26th.

Mr. O. A. WOOTTEN appeared for the defence.

The evidence taken on the previous occasion was read over.

In cross-examination by Mr WOOTTEN, prosecutor said on the day in question he did not get done until the afternoon. He did not call at one or two other public houses before coming into Cambridge. He had no other drink except that he had with prisoner at "Compasses."

Millie Chandler, widow, living in Compasses Passage, was called, but on being questioned by the CLERK said she had never seen the prisoner before.

The CLERK, said he must ask the Bench to allow Mrs Chandler to be treated as an adverse witness and cross-examined as to a statement she made to Detective Marsh.

The Bench assented, and the witness was cautioned that she was upon oath, the consequences of any false statement being pointed out to her. The Clerk: Do you remember talking with Marsh and White? —Witness: Yes.

Did you make a statement to them? —No, they asked the questions. I did not make a statement to them.

Do you swear you have never seen the prosecutor? —Never before, Sir.

I propose to read the statement you are alleged to have made to these two officers and I must again warn you to be very very careful. Did you not say to them "I live with Edward Hatley at the above address," that is 4, Compasses Passage? "On Thursday the 26 Dec., I was at home in the evening. The Prisoner was in my house. I left to fetch a loaf of bread and a bundle of wood. I only left for a few minutes. I do not know the time as I have no clock, but it was dark when I returned. I found the complainant in the house with my little boy and the prisoner Laxton. They had some beer. My little boy said complainant had given him a penny for fetching the beer. He did not give me anything and I never had any money from prisoner. I do not know what prisoner and complainant did. I know complainant left the house and the prisoner locked the door. He afterwards returned and I undid the door. He came in and said he had lost his money. I do not remember what else was said. Complainant might know me, as I have been over to Bottisham several times to visit friends, and he comes from there." Did you make that statement? —I did not.

The MAYOR: Of course you are fully aware of what you are now saying and the probable consequences of what you are saying if it is not true? —It is true.

And what you told the policeman is not true? — It is ——

The CLERK (interposing) what did you tell them? —Mr Marsh asked me a lot of questions I was not going to tell him. I knew nothing at all about it. I and Pattie Laxton, left that house, 4, Compasses Passage, between three and four. We went down to see a sister in New Street. It was something past eight when we went out again.

Do you say you never saw prosecutor? —I never saw him before.

Is the prisoner Fannie Laxton lodging with you? —Yes, Sir.

Mr WOOTTON: You were quite sober when the police came to you and when that alleged statement was made? — Yes, Sir.

Arthur Casbolt said he was a barman at the Rose and Crown, of which his father was licensee. On Friday, December 27, between eight and nine o'clock in the morning, he was in the bar. Prisoner came in with this woman Chandler. They called for two whiskies, which prisoner paid for. She put down half-a-

Continued

crown. They then went into the bar. Subsequently Edward Hatley and Charles Flack came in, and the prisoner called for two more whiskies which the men drank. Prisoner also paid for these drinks with a 2s. piece, which she took out of a purse. Witness saw into the purse and noticed some gold. Prisoner then called for a lemon and a beer. She drank the beer and Hatley had the lemon. Prisoner paid for these drinks. The party left the house together.

The MAYOR said the magistrate felt certain they could get further evidence if the case was again remanded, and it would therefore stand remanded for seven days.

WEDNESDAY

(Before the Mayor, G. Kett, Esq.; Dr. Cooper, and G. Smith, Esq.)

ASSAULT ON A WIFE —Walter Day, plasterer, of 16, Willow Place, appeared in answer to a warrant for assaulting his wife, Agnes Day, on November 19. — Defendant pleaded not guilty. — Complainant said on November 19 she was in her husband's house. Defendant was also there. He was drunk and started 'rounding' on her, using bad language. He next used bad language towards the children. Between seven and eight in the evening defendant threatened to knock her brains out with a stick. He had a stick in his hand and complainant put up her arm to ward off the blow, which fell on her hand. She told her husband she would not live with him, and she went out into the street, taking the children with her. Before going back she asked a policeman to watch near the house. She then returned with the two children. She saw nothing more of the defendant till the next evening. —By defendant: She broke a chair over his head in the afternoon when he kicked her. —Annie Goodman said on the day in question she was in Mrs Day's house. She saw defendant hit his wife with a stick. She had not seen complainant strike her husband before the assault. Defendant was drunk when the assault was committed.—By defendant: It was after complainant had been struck that she took the chair up. —By the Bench: Witness was not sure whether complainant hit her husband with the chair. —Acting Sergt. Wright said on Tuesday, about 6.10 p.m. he went to defendant's house. Witness asked him why he did not appear in answer to the summons served on him. He said he wasn't going to appear to make an exhibition of himself. She could take out 20 — ———— summonses; he shouldn't appear to them. Witness read the warrant which he had for defendant's arrest, and the latter then said "All right, I'll come, I shall be better looked after there than I shall be with her." —The Bench bound the defendant over to keep the peace for six months, himself in £5, and two sureties of £5 each. The alternative was a month's imprisonment. Defendant was also ordered to pay the costs, 18s.

SIX

A PUBLIC MEETING

In addition to his magisterial duties, there were of course public meetings to chair. Having already been troubled by the first of the two great evils, 'Politics', it was unfortunate that the very first public meeting Kett chaired as Mayor in January 1892 was concerned with the second, 'University Jurisdiction' at Cambridge.

Feelings against the University were running high and the Guildhall was packed by townspeople 'exceedingly partial towards speakers in favour of the total abolition of the powers possessed by the University over members not belonging to their own body.' Such feeling had been aroused in part by the case of Daisy Hopkins, accused of immoral behaviour. The case went to the Lord Chief Justice, who decided that she should be liberated but declined to certify for costs. The Cambridge Daily News reported 'He virtually said to her, "You have been wrongfully convicted; therefore I will commute your imprisonment for a fortnight into a fine of £100."' It promised to be an eventful evening.

Kett opened the meeting, and the audience received him warmly enough. 'I feel', Kett announced, 'this is a very important meeting for the reason that for many generations a feeling has existed between the two authorities of Cambridge – the University and Town – which, if it is possible in the future to soften down, would be of great benefit to all concerned.' As the audience cheered, Kett went on to stress his impartiality. 'In accepting the position of Chairman on this occasion it must not be assumed that I identify my personal sympathies either with or against the objects of this meeting; but to ensure a fair and impartial hearing for every speaker who might honour us with his feelings tonight.' Kett must have known that one of the hardest positions to assume when feelings are at boiling point is an impartial one.

As Chairman, Kett made the rule that although the mover of the first resolution might be allowed as much time as he required, each subsequent speaker should be limited to a maximum of fifteen minutes. On a characteristic note, Kett added that he felt 'If any good is to be done it will be from moderate and careful statements, and not from any extravagant or ill-natured remarks which might by accident be made.' He then called upon Dr Cooper to make the first resolution.

Dr Cooper had the pleasant task of being the People's Champion that night. His clever speech pleased and amused his audience so much that he could, at will, produce peals of laughter or shouts of outrage at the expense of the University Authorities. Himself a Town Councillor, Cooper began by throwing in a gently worded criticism that the Town Council allowed too few public meetings. 'We are assembled tonight in the good old constitutional way – a public meeting of the burgesses convened by our worthy Mayor; and I only wish such meetings were a more frequent occurrence. [Hear! Hear!] The reason why they are not is that the good people of the town are quite contented with its government and with the administration of the Town Council. [Hear! Hear!] But is has occurred to me that as there are many occasions when great public questions arise it would be returning with advantage to old times if we occasionally held public meetings to discuss public topics.' [Hear! Hear!]

Cooper's speech then focused on the subject of the debate; he told his audience that the University Proctors 'might break into any one of your houses, by night or day, without any warning, and all they have to say is 'We expected some evil.' [Cries of 'shame' from the audience.] 'Let the University give a proof', he bellowed, 'of their desire to live in harmony with the town by gracefully ceding the jurisdiction they possessed over the public amusements of the town. Why should the good people of the town, some thirty or forty thousand of them, be driven to other places for amusement simply because there was a chance of misbehaviour on the part of the University men.' [Hear, hear and cheers.]

Victorian students were under strict supervision from the Proctors, but of course some strayed and dallied in the town with prostitutes. These women if caught or suspected found themselves in the hated Spinning House.[6] Some students became drunk and disorderly after frequenting the town's pubs or joining in celebrations of the townsfolk. The University did its utmost to prevent recreation in the town and therefore tried to remove as many 'temptations' as they could from the students in their charge. They banned many planned public amusements.

The Old Police Station and Spinning House

The townspeople were full of anger and resentment. Cooper said, 'I would reduce the absurdity; there is nothing like doing that. When the University has organised a nice little concert of their own, and had all the arrangements complete; if I were Mayor, I would say, No, you do not get my consent.' He drew prolonged cheers from the audience. Cooper finished his speech with a personal plea. 'I appeal to you by all that you hold dear', he said, 'Pronounce with your voice that you will not any longer leave your homes, houses, wives and children to the mercy of the Proctors of the day.' The resolution was moved 'for the abolition or limitation of the powers possessed or exercised by the University to members of their own body.' Cooper left the platform amid storms of applause and cheers. The resolution was quickly seconded.

---

6 Spinning House, St Andrew's Street, demolished 1901. 'A receptacle for profligate and disorderly women'. In 1891 the Cambridge Daily News published a note – 'Funny Folks says, "What a 'reel' reform it would be if the institution known as the Spinning House could be wound up."'

At this point a Reverend Dixon rose and said he had a very modest amendment to put before them. The audience hissed. 'Kindly do not interrupt me until you know what it is', he said; and was about to go on when someone shouted, 'We don't want your amendment', whereupon the audience laughed and cheered. Dixon carried on, 'The amendment is this – that in the interests of the town it is desirable' – numerous cries of 'Sit down!', interrupted him but he went on, 'It is desirable that the special powers for dealing with the morality of Cambridge should not be taken away unless provision is made for the exercise of similar powers by some other lawfully constitued authority.' Now the audience overwhelmingly shouted 'No! No!' and hissed loudly and continuously.

Kett saw that things had already got out of hand; as Chairman and Mayor, it was his unenviable task to try to quieten the unruly crowd. He appealed to the audience to give the speaker a fair hearing. Dixon continued, 'I am very glad tonight to address an audience of Englishmen – a race of men who pride themselves on the love of fair play.' If he hoped to produce a response from that, he succeeded, but it was not the response he wanted. The uproar was very great, with liberal cries of 'Sit down' clearly heard above the clamour.

Kett again interrupted. 'We must protest against this unseemly behaviour. I ask you once more to give all speakers a fair hearing.' Someone shouted, 'I think they would listen to a townsman, Mr Mayor, but not a stranger.' Kett responded to this. 'I wish to remind this meeting that it is a meeting of the ratepayers of Cambridge, and that whether the ratepayers are members of the University or not, they are equally entitled to be here.' This produced more good-natured cheers, so the Reverend Dixon took courage to again essay the meeting, but he was greeted, amongst other cries, with 'Who shut the coffee tavern up?' It was not possible for him to speak. The Mayor rose as Dixon sat down, and Kett waited until the loud and prolonged cheers had subsided.

'I am extremely sorry that at my first appearance as Chairman of a meeting of this kind, my ruling for order should be so little regarded.' The audience subsided a little at this, but more amusement was to follow.

A Mr Vinter, evidently thinking that Reverend Dixon had exceeded the time allotted to each speaker, rose and endeavoured to address the Mayor. The uproar simply became greater, and the Reverend, finding that it was utterly impossible to make himself heard, placed some papers he held in his hand in his breast pocket and calmly folded his arms. Eventually he resumed his seat, and Vinter, finally addressing the Mayor, said 'I ask you to enforce the ruling that each speaker should be allowed a quarter of an hour.' The audience cheered. 'He has outraged every sense of decency in making the statements he has.' The audience were delighted.

Kett could not allow this. 'I must correct Mr Vinter as to the time that has been occupied by the last speaker. I made a careful note of the time, and I find that it was four minutes past nine when the last speaker addressed the meeting.' Although Reverend Dixon was then allowed four more minutes, he did not speak again except to sarcastically thank his audience.

Mr Spalding then arose, and was greeted with 'a perfect storm of hisses'. Kett reminded them that when the last speaker had attempted to address them, a person in the hall had said that if he had been a townsman, they would have heard him. 'Now you have a townsman', Kett continued, 'In the person of Mr Spalding, and I must beg you to hear him.' The response was 'No, No!' from the audience and the noise continued with even greater vigour.

Kett could see no possibility of matters improving: the townspeople would simply not hear a University representative. It was not possible to continue the meeting further. Kett was embarrassed and displeased. 'If a meeting is turned into a bear garden no good will come of it', he said, and the audience submitted with a few 'Hear hears'. 'You have given', Kett continued, 'a most impartial and fair hearing to one side only tonight, and I think that when you have a gentleman trying to address you it is a disgrace to Cambridge that these uproarious proceedings should take place.'

W. P. Spalding, taken during his term as Mayor (1910)

Finally the matter was put to the vote, although the Reverend's amendment was first considered. This was a mere formality since only 12 voted in favour of the amendment and 700 against. Lastly, the motion put forward so succinctly by Dr Cooper was carried with but a dozen dissentients.

The Conservative MP for Cambridge, Penrose Fitzgerald, addressed the meeting following the vote. 'If your Town Council and your Mayor, elected by the citizens of the town, in their wisdom and after hearing what the meeting had to say, consider it right to introduce into Parliament a Bill', said the MP in the traditional indirect and lengthy way, 'it is the duty of the representative not only to introduce the Bill, but to state its case as strongly as he could for his clients.' He was rewarded with loud cheers.

All that was left was for Kett to close the meeting, adding, 'I am very sorry that at my first public meeting of this character I was not better qualified to keep order.'

Although Kett was by no means the only Mayor not able to keep order at a public meeting,[7] he knew that the newspaper report would make good reading and that the whole town would discuss the 'turbulent proceedings'. But if he was dissatisfied, so were others. Two letters were sent to the Chronicle, one actually addressed to the Mayor not the Editor, and were speedily published. One of the letters is reproduced on the following page.

---

7 A public meeting in October 1893 was organised and plans to alter the front and rearrange the interior of the Guildhall were put before the rate-payers, who would not hear of it. Spalding tried to present the case, but the Chronicle reported, 'We have rarely seen Alderman subjected to so much opposition as that which Alderman Spalding had to withstand.' Alderman Kett also tried to present the merits of the scheme but had the sense to 'curtail his remarks in deference to the wishes to the audience'.

The following letter has been addressed to the Mayor of Cambridge

Cambridge, January 5, 1892

Dear MR MAYOR —The day before the meeting of Ratepayers to consider the action of the Town Council in the matter of the University Jurisdiction, I wrote to inform you that some of the Ratepayers who did not approve that action wished to attend; and that if it was proposed to lessen the existing special power of dealing with immorality here, two ratepayers other than myself would wish to propose and second an amendment and I might ask you to allow me to speak.

With the courtesy natural to you, you made excellent arrangements for our convenience. Before the meeting, I submitted to you the amendment, and I showed it to those who were to propose the resolution. All agreed that it was a perfectly fair and straightforward amendment. It was as follows:—

"That, in the interests of the town of Cambridge, it is desirable that the present special powers for dealing with immorality in Cambridge should not be taken away, unless provision is made for the exercise of similar powers by some other lawfully lawfully constituted authority."

Dr. J. W. Cooper, a barrister and a Magistrate of the Borough, the junior counsel for the applicant in the recent application for a writ of *habeas corpus*, professed to state to the meeting the facts respecting the legal authority and the exercise of the University Jurisdiction. On this statement of facts he claimed and received the support of the meeting for the resolution which, he moved in favour of the abolition of the Jurisdiction.

The meeting would not hear a Town Councillor when he corrected the first only of Dr. Cooper's statements of fact. For myself, I had carefully noted these statements, some of which were as far from the fact as positive language could make them. I have the experience of an old reporter, having myself reported all the debates in the Senate for twenty-one years. When I attempted to speak, having prefaced my remarks by a promise to lay before the meeting without reserve the information which I—as much, I suppose, as any living person—possess, I was stopped by the audience whenever I came to real business. You, who did all you could to induce them to behave decently, know that in word and tone and gesture I treated my audience with the patience and courtesy with which all previous Cambridge audiences, whether of the Town or the University, have treated me.

Under these circumstances I beg leave to send to you the following criticism of Dr. Cooper's statement of facts. And, as I was prevented from delivering it by the misconduct of the meeting, which treated you quite as disgracefully as it treated me, I propose to send copies to the newspapers. As there is not a town or district in the Kingdom which is not interested in the retention of the power of the University to protect these many hundreds of young men, only just emerged from the restraints of school or the seclusion of a country home, from the organised temptations of designing persons, I shall not confine myself to the local press.

I *a*. Dr. Cooper stated that the Jurisdiction rested on the confirmation of a Charter of Elizabeth by a Statute of Elizabeth. He said that when the Act was attained there was no public opinion brought to bear on the House of Commons, and that if a public press had been in existence at the time, no House of Commons would have thought of passing such an Act. The whole thing was obsolete, an obsolete jurisdiction, an obsolete Statute, and as such he demanded its repeal.

I *b*. The answer is that in 1854 and 1855 the University and the Town went carefully through conditions of their mutual relations; concessions were made; an agreement was arrived at under Sir John Patteson's arbitration; and both parties found themselves under seal to keep the Award. In 1856, when there certainly was a public opinion and a public press, an Act of Parliament was passed to confirm this Award. The enactment which stands in the forefront of the Act of 1856 is this '*VI The Power of the University exercised by the Proctors shall be continued as it now by Law exists.*' If that is not recent enough, changes were made in the arrangements in 1889. In that year the Town and University agreed to the terms of an Order by the Local Government Board. An Act of Parliament was passed to confirm this Order and Section VI of the Award Act was among the arrangements kept in force.

Dr. Cooper knows all this as well as I do. He not only suppressed even the faintest allusion to it, but he assured his audience that the whole thing was an obsolete Charter and Statute of three hundred years ago.

II *a*. Dr. Cooper said 'The University can break into the house of any one of you at any hour of night or day and all they'd have to say is that they suspected evil.'

II *b*. The first instruction I received many years ago ran thus: – 'You have the right to search houses of ill fame. But you must never attempt to break into a house of ill fame.'

III *a*. Dr. Cooper said that in the Vice-Chancellor's Court (meaning before last autumn,

Continued

when the procedure was changed at the request of the Town Council) no witnesses were called.

II *b*. As many witnesses were called as would suffice in a police court. In many of the ordinary police cases two constables are the only witnesses. The Vice-Chancellor has taken the evidence of the Proctor and two constables.

IV *a*. Dr. Cooper said no evidence was taken on oath.

IV *b*. It has been entirely in the power of the Vice-Chancellor to hear evidence on oath or not on oath. In the last 25 years, beyond which my experience does not go, some Vice-Chancellors have in all cases administered oaths; some have exercised their discretion according to conditions of the case; some have never found it necessary to administer an oath.

V *a*. Dr. Cooper said that charges, found a name in it, said it was hers, and proceeded to try her as being that woman, whatever her name might really be.

V *b*. I believe that under the circumstances it is not libellous to say that this is ludicrously false. It was given as a positive and general fact, and with a wealth of objectionable phrase and tense.

VI *a*. Dr. Cooper roused indignation against the Vice-Chancellor's Court by contrasting it with Courts where not a word is said of previous convictions until the prisoner is found guilty of the new charge.

VI *b*. In the Borough Magistrates' Court we always used to have a complete statement of previous convictions and penalties, before ever the prisoner appeared in court at all, and it was in our hands throughout the hearing. The Vice-Chancellor has had exactly that and nothing more.

I say, 'We used to have,' for I was some time ago prevented by a sense of self-respect by continuing to sit on the Cambridge Bench. The great majority of my brother magistrates, it is right to add after that remark, are men whom it is a pleasure to meet anywhere.

VII *a*. Dr. Cooper assured his audience on the facts he has stated to them; that he did not exaggerate or overstate any part of the case; and that he would be followed by Members of the University who would correct him if they could.

VI *b*. I followed him; but I was not allowed to correct him. I now do so.

It is characteristic of the proceedings that another Borough Magistrate, Mr. Balls, speaking of the courtesy with which he and his fellow delegates from the Town Council had been received by the representatives of the Council of the Senate, of whom I was one, requited that courtesy by rousing the groans of the audience with the assertion that no concessions were made. The fact is that the Vice-Chancellor on that occasion asked the Mayor to state the objections felt by the Town Council. The Mayor stated three. He was then interrupted by some of his own colleagues, who continued the proceedings on their own lines. All of the three points mentioned by the Mayor were conceded. They were, (1) That the Vice-Chancellor's Court should be open, (2) That evidence should (always, I suppose) be taken on oath, (3) That the prisoner should have legal advice if she wished it (it had never been refused in our memory).

Had I been allowed to fulfil my promise of full information, I should have added that the prisoner, from the moment of entering the Spinning House on the night of arrest, is in the hands of women alone, a fact the importance of which cannot be over-rated. Also, that her friends were always sent to at once, if she wished it, and that at times, they have been present at the hearing; I remember one case in particular where the prisoner's uncle entreated the Vice-Chancellor to keep her locked up. Also, that no prisoner has asked for a legal adviser; the cases have been quite clear, and the unfortunate women have desired to have everything conducted as quietly as possible. In their own better interest; and in the interest of public decency, I have entirely agreed with them.

That the powers of the Proctors have been exercised in a considerate and forbearing manner, the delegates of the Town Council, in answer to my direct question, directly allowed. I myself, as one of the six Proctors and Pro-proctors in office at a time, arrested 17 persons in 18 terms, throwing all my endeavours into driving temptation out of the streets, which the police cannot do, and only arresting when preventive action failed.

That every sensible man would agree with Lord Coleridge that this jurisdiction is most important to be kept up, the Chief Justice in delivering judgment last month said in the strongest way was his opinion.

I have the honour to be, Mr. Mayor, your very obedient fellow townsman
G. F. BROWNE

Magistrate for the Borough, Alderman of the County Council for Cambridgeshire; Disney Professor in the University and Member of the Council of the Senate; and Canon of St. Paul's.

To George Kett, Esquire, Mayor of Cambridge

A few weeks later a brief paragraph mentioned that the University's jurisdiction remained in the town, yet as a result of amicable negotiations between the authorities, the rights of the University were surrendered to civil authorities in 1894.

SEVEN

SIGNIFICANT EVENTS IN CAMBRIDGE

During January 1891 the killer disease influenza began to spread in the town and on the 11th of that cold month the Duke of Clarence, Prince Albert Victor[8] (the Prince of Wales' heir) died in London. The whole country fell into official mourning, the Corporation attending a special service at St Paul's Church. Shopkeepers, on this occasion without exception, suspended business, and the streets thronged with people assembled to watch the Mayor's procession which was headed by four mace bearers, the maces draped in black. Spectators awaited their arrival at St Paul's on Hills Road, all of them (according to the Chronicle's reporter) 'appearing to recognise the solemnity of the occasion.' The death of the Duke of Clarence may not have affected ordinary people much, beyond the day of the funeral, but for those who had a social life the event was solemn indeed, since it prevented social high-jinks and party gatherings for a portion of the coming season. Closer to home, the papers reported every day on a new case of the disease afflicting a prominent person, and the death columns were well-filled.

Improvement of services

To lighten the city's gloom, in the following month Cambridge Corporation was granted £25,840 by the local government board for the first installation of electric light in the town. The Corporation's original request had been for £35,000. The amount accepted was considered to be too small, and only parts of the city could benefit. The efficiency of the gas lamps tested in January 1899 was equivalent to the light emitted by approximately 15 candles.

Electricity had arrived, but was not installed in most of the houses, even the grander ones, until many years later. For the first two years the use of electricity was strictly limited for illumination purposes in public places after dark. Electricity was installed in St Paul's church in 1904.

Communication was improving, too. The first telephone trunk line from Cambridge to London was opened on 20 June 1886. Rattee and Kett had one of the early three digit numbers.

Health

In the late nineteenth century Cambridge, like other towns during Victorian times, was plagued by potentially fatal diseases such as smallpox, measles, whooping cough, typhoid and diarrhoea. During 1884 it was the last of these afflictions which caused the most fatalities, claiming 28 lives. It was during this year that the infectious diseases hospital or sanatorium was established in Mill Road.

---

8 Albert Victor, Duke of Clarence (1864–92). Rumours abound – he is said to have married secretly during the 1880s: to have fallen in love with a Roman Catholic; and has even been suspected of being Jack the Ripper! He was engaged to Princess May of Teck but died before the marriage.

The Town Council's Sanatorium Committee was responsible for the sanatorium, where the beds increased from six in 1888 to 62 in 1915. Visitors in 1886 were advised:

a   Not to enter any of the wards when in a weak state of health.

b   To partake of food before entering the hospital.

c   To avoid touching the patient or exposing themselves to the breath or emanations from the skin.

d   To sit some distance from the patient.

e   Not to enter any railway carriage or other public conveyance immediately after leaving the hospital.

f   To wear wrappers, provided by the hospital, to cover their dress when in the wards, and to wash their hands with carbolic soap before leaving the hospital.

Although these rules made good common sense, imagine being a patient – or a visitor!

During one of the regular meetings of the Town Council in 1898, the Sanatorium Committee came under fire and was asked for an explanation of the £7 12s 3d spent on ale and brandy for the sanatorium. Councillor Hills said he believed brandy was used for patients and there was no excess in that respect. The amount of beer drunk was in bottles, not casks, and 'as there have been more nurses at the sanatorium recently, more has been drunk'. Noticing an extra item, Councillor Wootten asked, 'Do nurses drink sloe gin as well?' 'That', replied Hills, 'was ordered by a doctor for a particular patient supposed to be suffering from typhoid fever.'

The Sanatorium became Brookfields Hospital in 1948, and the infectious diseases wards transferred to Addenbrookes Hospital in 1973. Brookfields became a geriatric hospital after this date.

Laws

Kett served not only on the Town Council, but was for ten years also a County Councillor. The Mayor therefore took his place as ordinary Councillor at an autumn meeting of the Cambridge County Council. One of the items on the agenda was the wording of certain bye-laws.

It was proposed that 'yelling' and 'hooting' in the street should be an offence, but it was suggested the words should be removed from the bye-law. 'It might prove a dangerous thing at election time. We might find half the constituency locked up!' The terms of the bye-law, it was pointed out, were dangerously wide, and one Councillor wanted to see 'abusive, insulting or threatening language removed'. Kett agreed thoroughly and seconded the amendment, but it was rejected with a large majority. 'It will be very valuable to solicitors and council', felt the majority. Kett, as Chief Magistrate, found the bye-law irritating and wanted to avoid such trivial behaviour being expanded into a matter for the court.

Business

Although he must have relied heavily on George Robert and Edmund, George Kett was still very much in control of Rattee and Kett. The lease for the Station Road premises came up for renewal in October 1891 – the site belonged to Jesus College – and Kett replied personally, agreeing with the terms.

Dear Sir

I only returned to Cambridge last evening after a few days' absence and find your letter of the 17th. I will send the Bursar's letter containing the conditions as accepted for the new lease. Please note that Mr William Kett's name is now to be omitted from the new lease, as he is in no way interested in the matter, having retired from business and premises in which he has had no interest for several years past.

Yours faithfully,

George Kett

The present owners are: George Kett, Edmund Kett and Alfred Kett.

The lease was renewed for 40 years from 29 September 1891. Terms: Fine[9] including expenses, £170; rent for first 20 years £8; for last 14 years £16 13s 4d.

When November arrived, family and business pressures forced Kett to refuse office for a further year. In a speech of thanks to the retiring Mayor, Alderman Wace said, 'I am sure we all regret Alderman Kett has been obliged to decline the honour of serving the office for another year.' Nichols, who had been against Kett's election, added now that Kett's 'unvarying kindness and courtesy has been most marked, and everyone must have seen it and known it. Sincere thanks are due not just from the Town Council, but from the town at large.'

A notice appeared in the Chronicle commending Kett's year of office, and commenting on the ill-health of Catherine which had overshadowed the whole year for the Mayor. 'We regret, together with the whole town, that Alderman Kett's year of office should have been darkened by severe family affliction, but at the same time the knowledge that he had the sympathy of all was a source of no little consolation to Mr Kett.'

Kett's reply was characteristically short. 'So far as social matters are concerned, I have not been able to carry out that part of the programme to my own satisfaction.' Typically, there was one aspect of the Mayoralty that Kett had treated with priority; 'I hope that all business matters have been handled to everyone's approval', he said – and on that point the Council members, of both parties, could only agree.

George Kett was 56 years old in 1892, but his capacity for work was undiminished. Freed of the duties of Mayor, he continued to work zealously on behalf of the town and on his own behalf.

Family

The arrival of long-awaited grandson, George, brightened 1891, and the birth of Reginald George Robert in 1892 and Edmund August in 1893 balanced the sexes. At this point there were three healthy grandsons to compliment the three elder grand-daughters; similarly there had been pleasing symmetry when George Kett's own children had been born, all of whom had been strong and healthy.

In 1894, the Kett's youngest son Frederick William married Ellen Preston, of Cherry Hinton; but the wedding celebrations were quelled by the untimely death of Catherine Sarah, George and Catherine's eldest daughter, on 9 April. She died soon after giving birth to her second son at Lowestoft – her other child was just two years old.

George and Catherine brought their daughter's body home to Cambridge, and buried her at Mill Road Cemetery. Her gravestone reads 'In loving remembrance of Catherine Sarah, wife of Reginald John Roberts MD. Born at Cambridge, August 23rd 1863, died at Lowestoft April 9th 1894. Eldest daughter of George and Catherine Kett.'

The Kett's two young grandsons were not without a replacement mother for long. Dr Roberts married his dead wife's younger sister, Alice Caroline, two years later in 1896.

9 Fee

The marriage would have been illegal in England at that time, so the couple were married in Jersey and settled afterwards on the Isle of Wight. The family approved of the match, since they felt that there could be no-one better to look after the two little boys than their Aunt Alice. Dr and the new Mrs Roberts and family were recalled to Cambridge every Christmas; and the grandchildren were photographed in the garden at Wymondham House on a sunny day in July 1897.

Sadly, Catherine Sarah's sons died young – the eldest, named after her husband, died when he was five years old; and the youngest, Gerald Kett Roberts, at fifteen, in a training accident at the Royal Naval College, Dartmouth. Both boys were buried in Cambridge. Alice had one son, Peter, born in 1899.

Back row (l to r): Trixie, Catherine, Hilda
Seated: George with Edmund and Gerald, Catherine, Reginald and George
(sitting cross-legged).

EIGHT

RATTEE & KETT EXPANDS

Geeorge Kett had realised for some time that the business premises on Station Road were simply not large enough for the ever-increasing work load. He had been looking for a new site, and found a piece of land for sale that was ideal for his purpose. His offer for the land, which belonged to Jesus College, was accepted, and Kett was ready to set up a second premises in Cambridge immediately. However, the transaction for the Purbeck Road site was to prove not as simple as that.

£1,200 was the sum agreed upon in 1895. There was a tenant already on the site, a Mr Solly, who apparently knew he was well within his rights to refuse to leave immediately.

Jesus College solicitors Francis & Francis reported in a letter that they had seen Mr Kett, 'Who considers that he purchases for immediate possession and he therefore declines to enter into any negotiations with the present tenant Mr Solly.' Kett, in a hurry to move, decided it was cheaper to offer compensation to Mr Solly in the hope of getting possession. 'We have seen Mr Kett', wrote Francis & Francis on 3 August, 'He is willing to give £15 by way of compensation with a view to gaining possession by Michaelmas. We have therefore written to Mr Solly to offer him £25 [£10 was to come from the College]. 'We will let you know as soon as we receive his reply.'

Mr Solly, however, was not so easily removed. On 13 November 1895, another letter to Jesus College, this time from Charles Bidwell, confirms the difficulties.

> 'I have this morning met Mr Solly and Mr Kett on the ground and marked out the road and the three acres. Mr Kett is very anxious that the road should be made at once, and that Mr Solly should remove all his buildings which stand on that road. Mr Kett expresses surprise, that where possible the road should not have been set out 36 foot wide, as this is the narrowest road, sanctioned by under corporation bye-laws, to front houses to.'

Kett's reference to the bye-law seems like a threat.

Mr Solly refused to move his buildings. The date of 29 September came and went, and it transpired that Mr Solly had a right to possession until Michaelmas 1897! The solicitors were clearly struggling, but a solution was finally reached when Mr Solly was awarded a substantial sum of £66 10s 0d by Jesus College.

It was all very irritating for Kett, who finally withdrew his offer of £15 to Mr Solly because of the delay, although he still agreed to pay £10 towards the payment to Solly made by the College. It was April 1896 before Kett finally obtained possession of the land. The land was next to the railway, essential for delivering the large blocks of heavy stone and wood which were the raw materials of the trade. There were workshops to build, more men to employ, the premises and numerous sites around the country to organise – more than enough to keep all the Ketts busy. The site at Purbeck Road still remains today.

Grandson George with one of the Rattee & Kett vehicles.

Sketch of the restoration work at Arundel Castle, 1904

NINE

JUBILEE YEAR

Queen Victoria's Diamond Jubilee was celebrated all over the country, and Kett became heavily involved in the organisation of events in Cambridge. There was glorious weather in June 1897, and the events spanned a whole sunny week. Naturally it all began with the Corporation attending a very lengthy service at church on Sunday, and on Monday the fun really began. There was a smoking concert,[10] and there was a competition for decorated bicycles, with prizes going to the most original costumes and machines. The winner was a Mr W Dunn of Chesterton, and this is the description of his bike: 'it was covered with flowers, ornamental grass, a stag's head, and Chinese lanterns, and over the back wheel there was a stuffed monkey. The competitor wore the dress of an Indian sportsman.' Unfortunately, there is no photograph!

On Tuesday there were gun salutes and hundreds of pigeons were set loose. A luncheon at the Guildhall was attended not by George but by George Robert. In the afternoon a trapeze artist and an acrobat entertained the crowds on Parker's Piece, repeating their programme of entertainment in the evening. There were sports, and a handicapper had been hard at work organising the boy's races, since some started from 'scratch', while some had a 70 yards start.

Decorated carriages were another attraction, and of course the procession – Kett sat with the important members of the Corporation in one of the first two carriages. 'Laughter holding on both sides reigned supreme on Market Hill as the procession dispersed, and the Mayor (Horace Darwin) and Corporation laughed and made merry on a municipal scale', wrote the Chronicle's reporter. A pretend 'fire and rescue' was another attraction on Market Hill, while on the river there was a water carnival and boat races. Bands played continuously, a concert was organised in the Guildhall, and street illuminations and decorations were everywhere.

Citizens of Victorian Cambridge certainly knew how to celebrate, and today's events, popular though they are, can only be an echo of those of yesteryear. 'There was hardly a single item which did not have a counter-attraction', gloated the Chronicle. The old people were given a free dinner, there were treats for the children, and a grand dinner for the inmates of the workhouse.

---

10 Unaware of the dangers of tobacco, smoking was extremely fashionable but only for men. In almost every photograph of George Robert a cigarette appears in his hand or mouth, and a photograph of grandson George with his two sisters shows him smoking at the age of 12 or thereabouts.

The flags are out for Queen Victoria's Jubilee, 1897, Kings Parade, Cambridge

TEN

THE SUPERLATIVE YEARS

On 11 November 1898, the Cambridge Town Council gathered at the Guildhall for the purpose of electing the new Mayor. Alderman Hills put forward the proposal. 'I take it as a great honour to be called upon to propose the name of a gentleman to fill the high office of Mayor for the Borough for the ensuing year. My task is a very easy one', Hills enthused, 'but to no-one does it give greater pleasure than to myself. You will understand just how easy my task is when I mention the name of Mr George Kett.' The Councillors responded with applause. Hills went on; 'There is no need for me to recommend Alderman Kett to the favourable notice of the Council. Mr Kett has been a resident of Cambridge for the past 30 years, and during this period he has shown his powers of organisation and management by developing and controlling a large and increasingly prosperous business.' The compliments continued; 'I believe he is a man of integrity, business-like, level-headed and I believe without an enemy, at any rate within the Council.' Hills then made a reference to the fiasco of the inauguration of the previous Mayor seven years before. 'Mr Kett is starting under more favourable auspices than in 1891. Then there was no understanding between the two political parties in the Council on the election of the Mayor, and so Mr Kett found himself to be more Mayor of a party than of a Council. However, his capability and impartiality, added to his hospitable and social qualities, soon removed that impression and now, elected by the unanimous voice of the Council, we wish him health, happiness and good fortune during his second year as Mayor.' Hills stopped for the applause, and added, 'Perhaps the greatest compliment we could pay Mr Kett is to assume everyone knows him, and his great qualifications for the post.'

Hills sat down and various other Councillors keenly spoke of Kett's qualities. One point was especially made by Dr Porter. The University of Cambridge was due to confer an honorary degree on 'our great military hero, Lord Kitchener', and for the very first time the Mayor was invited to take part in the proceedings. There were to be great steps made in the co-operation between 'Town and Gown' in Kett's second year as Mayor.

In response to his election as Mayor, Kett rose to make the customary speech. It was a totally different experience to that of 1891, and Kett even allowed a light bantering to creep into his speech of thanks, teasing Hills for his over-flattering words.

Council business swiftly got underway. Kett began his second term of office, looking forward perhaps to the forthcoming celebration that was already on most people's minds – the visit of Lord Kitchener to Cambridge just thirteen days away.

Kitchener at Cambridge

24 November 1898 was a bitterly cold day. The people of Cambridge crowded the streets near the Guildhall in order to catch a glimpse of Lord Kitchener, the war hero of this period. He had just returned from his victory at Omdurman two months before. This success enabled the British to gain control of the Sudan, and the highest honours were

conferred on Kitchener. He was made a Baron and awarded £30,000. Cambridge also wanted to heap honours on the country's hero, and Kitchener had come to the town to receive the Freedom of the Borough and an Honorary Degree.

However history might judge the great colonial war commanders, to the vast majority of people at the time they really were heros. Most Victorians were wildly patriotic and victory at war was regarded as glorious. The displays of flags and bunting, the cheers and the honours, confirmed that Cambridge people were as enthusiastic as any Victorians could be; they were well prepared to receive their hero, to enjoy and remember his visit for a long time to come. 'This was done', reported the Chronicle, 'in no niggardly spirit.'

His Lordship arrived on the 10.45 am train. Although his arrival time had been kept a secret a crowd had assembled at the station to welcome him. Lord Kitchener was wearing civilian clothes, although he changed into full military uniform later. An outburst of cheering greeted Kitchener outside the station, where a carriage drawn by two horses was waiting to transport him to Christ's College. His walk across the court to the Master's Lodge was accompanied by a hearty ovation from the surrounding crowds.

At the Master's Lodge, George Kett (Mayor), Alderman Ginn (Deputy Mayor) and JEL Whitehead (Town Clerk) were introduced to Lord Kitchener. Kett and his entourage then returned to the Guildhall, where there was much activity. At 11 o'clock the guard of honour had paraded in Parson's Court and then marched via Peas Hill to Market Hill. Immediately facing the main entrance inside a roped-off area the band of the Battalion were playing their selection of music. The front portion of the Guildhall was barricaded and the steps were carpeted. A profusion of palms and plants crowded the vestibule, and rugs and drapery hid the 'unattractive walls' from view.

Inside the crimson-carpeted hall, the Mayor and Alderman arrived to take their places on the platform, where a seat was ready for the Sirdar[11] . Admission to the public was secured by tickets – and the orchestra and gallery, in addition to the hall, were crowded with spectators. Many local important people were present – representatives from both the town and the University. Among those noticed by the Chronicle's eagle-eyed reporter was George Robert Kett. His father requested people to keep their seats until after the ceremony and the Sirdar and members of the Council had left the hall.

Lord Kitchener arrived amidst cheers at 12.15. The noise almost drowned the words of the Town Clerk as he read the minutes authorising the admittance of Lord Kitchener to the honorary freedom of the Borough.

The schedule was tight; the Town Clerk's speech was full of compliments and admiration but was not over-long, and the Mayor soon handed over the casket containing the Freedom of the Borough and the address which bore his signature to Lord Kitchener. Kitchener's speech of thanks was also brief. 'I have to express to you my very sincere thanks for the high honour you have done me in admitting me into the freedom of this ancient Borough and also for the very flattering address in this very beautiful casket, which I shall always prize very dearly.' The public applauded wildly. The Sirdar and the Mayor left the hall together, whereupon Kitchener took leave of Kett to travel to Downing College where he lunched with the Vice-Chancellor.

Before Kitchener's arrival at Downing College, undergraduate students in the gallery had begun bantering with the older generation beneath. Then a length of hose was found, and a stream of water gently descended on those below who naturally thought it a one-sided joke. The students sang popular military songs, 'The Soldiers of the Queen' and 'A Little British Army', to keep the time from dragging.

Kitchener's arrival was greeted with enthusiasm, but the Public Orator, Dr Sandys, had a harder time. At the end of 'one of his well-balanced periods', someone mournfully chimed 'the *sands* of time are sinking', and another, suggesting that Kitchener might share his aversion to classics, quipped, 'You 'aves to 'ave it whether you like it or not!.'

When the speeches were over, the relieved students, sang 'For He's a Jolly Good

11 Kitchener was often known as Sirdar as he held the title of Director General of the Egyptian Army.

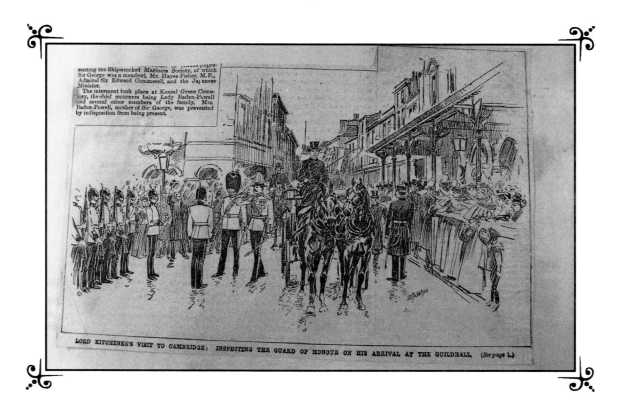

senting the Shipwrecked Mariners Society, of which
Sir George was a member), Mr. Hayes Fisher, M.P.,
Admiral Sir Edward Commerell, and the Japanese
Minister.

The interment took place at Kensal Green Ceme-
ry, the chief mourners being Lady Baden-Powell
nd several other members of the family. Mrs.
Baden-Powell, mother of Sir George, was prevented
by indisposition from being present.

LORD KITCHENER'S VISIT TO CAMBRIDGE: INSPECTING THE GUARD OF HONOUR ON HIS ARRIVAL AT THE GUILDHALL. (See page L.)

The strain proved too great, and a few minutes before
the Sirdar's arrival several yards of these railings fell
upon the pavement crushing a half-dozen persons.

THE SIRDAR AT CAMBRIDGE: THE MAYOR PRESENTING THE FREEDOM TO LORD KITCHENER IN THE GUILDHALL.

Sketches from the 'Daily Graphic' November 25 1898.

Fellow'. Kitchener found upon leaving by carriage that his ordeal was by no means over. It was traditional for students to unharness the horses from a hero's carriage and then draw it through the streets themselves. The students packed together to form a crowd so dense and so enthusiastic that the fore part of his carriage was broken away. The Sirdar is reported to have put up with this over-zealous admiration with 'great good humour'.

In the late afternoon, Kitchener attended a special meeting at the Union Rooms where he become an honorary member of the society. In the evening, he dined with the Master of Christ's College and attended a reception afterwards at the Lodge.

More unscheduled entertainment amused the undergrads during the night. Gangs of them – some in groups of up to 200 in number – scoured the town for wood to fuel a celebration bonfire held on Market Hill. The Chronicle reported: 'Unfortunately they did not confine themselves to taking all the empty boxes they could find, but hand carts, valuable building materials, young trees, garden fences, goal posts – in fact every movable thing was taken and thrown onto the fire. The band pavilion on Christ's Pieces was partially wrecked and all the music stands were used as fuel.' In addition, 'The Town Hall clock and the windows of several of the houses formed targets for many of the undergraduates. Few could hit the clock, but unfortunately many windows were broken.' It was well into the night before the bonfire began to die down and the intense heat smashed the glass in two of the lamps near the conduit. The debris from the fire filled many cartloads.

One thing is certain, the Mayor took a dim view of the proceedings. Although the students were outside his jurisdiction, the matter of repairing the town's property certainly was not. To Kett, who favoured only 'moderate and careful statements', and to many of the townsfolk, the behaviour of the students must have been very galling indeed.

ELEVEN

TOWN AND GOWN AGAIN

Two weeks after the town and the University had joined forces to welcome Kitchener, the members of the Corporation were invited to meet the Vice-Chancellor of the University at dinner. 'Saturday', trumpeted the Chronicle on 9 December 1898, 'was a red letter day.' 'Never before' had such an event taken place. The occasion signified the kind of co-operation between the town and the University which would have been impossible a few years before. Since the Local Government Act of 1889 the University was represented on the Town Council by six Councillors (out of a total of 36), two of whom were Aldermen.

The Lord Mayor of Birmingham who had graduated from Cambridge University 35 years before and was leader of a town 'twelve times' the size of Cambridge, was also invited. He was seated on the right hand of the Vice-Chancellor while Kett was seated to the left of the Vice-Chancellor.

The after-dinner speeches focused on the value of University education. The Lord Mayor pointed out, 'There is a natural feeling that municipal life is a thing for a man who wants personal advancement, and that it is not quite the thing for educated men to go into the Council.' Later he said, 'I am always glad when a noble lord is induced to accept the office of Mayor of the City. It might be that a noble lord would not always be able to do the detailed work that municipal life put before him, but his action showed the country that municipal life was a thing that any man might be proud to embark on.' He went on, 'I do not think you want a council composed entirely of educated men. I believe no town could really have the whole confidence of the community unless all classes of the community are represented in it. So we find upon these bodies professional men, manufacturers, shopkeepers and, lastly, representatives of the working classes. Formerly we used to be very much afraid of the working classes getting upon the governing bodies; we did not know what disturbances might arise, and it was not unnatural that we should have timidity in that respect. But we have found the representatives of the working classes in Birmingham have been of the greatest possible use, and, so far from being afraid of them, we take care they are put on all committees where their services could be of greatest service to the city.'

Kett's own brief speech focused upon the value of the University members within the Council. 'It is very evident that in the selection of representatives made by the University, they have chosen not the drones of the university but the working bees.' It was a genuine sentiment, for the University representatives had worked hard within the various committees. Kett thanked the Vice-Chancellor for his hospitality and hoped that the good relations between Town and Gown would strengthen; but he said little else.

Rowland Parker[12] tells of an instance of 'stupid snobbery', which must, he felt, be a 'hangover from the nineteenth century. Just before the First World War, a University don and his wife met a well-to-do Cambridge couple on holiday at an east coast resort and

---

12 Rowland Parker 'Town and Gown – the 700 years war'.

spent a pleasant fortnight in their company at the same boarding house. On the morning of their departure, the don's wife said to the other lady, 'It has been very nice meeting you, but of course we shall not know you when we are back in Cambridge. You're not University.'

In spite of these kinds of sentiments, Kett continued to sign his business letters 'George Kett – Builder'. When elected as a Director of the Cambridge Water Company (another Town and Gown amalgamation), he gave his occupation as 'Builder' which indicates that he was in no way ashamed of his trade. No titled man was ever more proud of his family history than Kett. His ancestors had been celebrated leaders of men; and if Kett did encounter any Victorian class snobbery, he was apparently untroubled by it.

TWELVE

WOMEN

Women had a distinct position in the background of all but the most progressive and modern families and education for women was still confined to the middle and upper classes. 'A woman's place is in the home' was a popular Victorian sentiment.[13] The male attitude towards women is demonstrated by a remark made by Alderman Ginn at the University-Corporation dinner. Talking about the University being open to all classes of society (which of course it wasn't) he said, 'We might, in 50 years' time for instance, see women admitted to degrees.' The all-male assembly laughed since this was a topical joke. Proposals that degrees should be awarded to women were defeated in 1888 and again in 1896-7. In 1896, a poll in the Cambridge Review revealed that the undergraduates voted 1,723 to 446 against the proposal. In 1897 the result was 1,707 against and 661 in favour. Women acquired equal status 49 years later. Ironically Alderman Ginn's prediction was actually almost exactly correct!

Although the Spinning House came under Civil authority in 1894 (and was demolished in 1901), another organisation existed for the containment of women of low moral standards; the institute was called the Cambridge Female Refuge. In December 1898 Kett was invited, as Mayor, to chair the annual meeting of this association. Those who gathered in the Alderman's Parlour were mainly church men, with a few representatives from the Town Council, along with a reporter from the Chronicle.

There were twenty-six girls at the home, all of whom were expected to show suitable gratitude for being allowed to reside there. In 1897, five of their number had left to enter into service (this was the best that could be hoped for them and was considered a triumph); two had been dismissed from the refuge; one had returned home and another sent to a different Refuge. Nine new girls had replaced them.

How the girls had come to lose their 'virtue' was not considered although this was obviously sometimes unjust. Anyone who showed charity towards such creatures were considered extremely tolerant. Many preferred to pretend that such people didn't exist; or that if they did, they did not deserve charity.

The end-of-year report describes life within the Refuge. 'The training of the inmates in laundry and household work has carried on as usual. It is very satisfactory that the girls should do so much to earn their own living and not be wholly dependent on the charity of others. The amount of washing done during the year by a comparatively small number of girls is very creditable [sic] to the excellent management of the Matron and the industry of the girls themselves. Care is taken that the hours of work should not be

---

13 Compare, for example, the contents of the Girls' Own and Boys' Own papers as published in the Chronicle in October 1892. Girls' Own paper considers 'What to do with your savings', 'On helping in the house', and 'Flower decorations for October'. Boys' Own paper on the other hand, published 'thrilling stories of actual adventure intermingled with fiction of equal interest, then all games which boys love, football, cricket, bowls are explained and interesting anecdotes furnished of eminent players. Boys are helped to conjure, carpenter, and make knick-knacks ad-lib.'

excessive, and that inmates should have some variety of entertainment and a reasonable amount of recreation. In return for their labours the girls had three pence a week after they had been in the home six months, and the sum increased as time went on.'

After listening to the report, Kett responded with his speech. 'When I was asked to take the Chair at this meeting a few weeks ago I readily consented to do so. The institution was founded, I believe, exactly 60 years ago. I myself have lived in the parish in which the building is situated for the past 50 years. I am ashamed to say, coming to the meeting as Chairman, I know little of the work of the institution. The only excuse I can offer is that the work carries on so quietly, and almost secretly, that few outside those who took a deep interest in the institution could know of its existence. We are glad to see in the report a record of so much good work done in the home. The Refuge is fortunate in its Matron who is willing to exercise a happy, moral influence on those under her charge. That is proved by the fact that when the girls leave the home they take pleasure in visiting their old mistress, whom they have learnt to love and respect. I am pleased to read in the report that an annual excursion is an institution connected with the refuge. It occurs to me that the expenses attending that outing would cheerfully be met if the Refuge was better known in the town. The outing is one of the few things in their lives that the girls can look forward to. I think that if the Refuge could be more generally known, more sympathy would be felt and considerably more interest taken in its welfare. In the meantime thanks are due to those ladies and gentlemen who have shown so much fortitude in carrying on quiet and useful work in the interests of those poor wretches who are, humanly speaking, quite unable to help themselves out of the mire into which they have fallen.'

Kett's speech was genuinely one of concern and kindness, but typically Victorian. Women especially were not only struggling to achieve an improved position in society but were more likely to be judged by the hypocritical and obsessive attitude the Victorians had towards 'morality'. It was more convenient to label the inmates of the Refuge as 'fallen' and 'unable to help themselves' than to scrutinise the reasons why they found themselves in these circumstances.

THIRTEEN

ENTERTAINMENT

The Mayor's duties were not confined to the Chairing of innumerable meetings. There was also a social aspect to his job. On 16 December Kett graced the Cambridge Conservative Club (of which he was Trustee) with his presence at their 'At Home'. This event was an 'animated and brilliant scene with an excellent programme of music, recitations and conjuring', which began at 8.30 pm and finished at 11 pm. Once Catherine's health improved she was able to take her place as Mayoress. She usually accompanied her husband on these social occasions, and Kett's great reputation for hospitality would have been due, at least in part, to his wife's efforts. Maud Mary also participated at various functions, while George Robert was a great help. He worked full-time with his brother Edmund at Rattee and Kett, and also took an interest in municipal affairs.

George Kett and his wife also entertained on a grand scale. An example of the Kett's hospitality is found in a report published in the Chronicle on 28 July 1899.

THE MAYOR'S GARDEN PARTIES

The Mayor and Mayoress of Cambridge on Wednesday entertained a large company in the 'Fellows' Gardens of Trinity College. Indeed the invitations sent out were so numerous that the function resolved itself into two parties, one in the afternoon the other in the evening. The Fellows' Gardens at Trinity lend themselves most admirably to such gatherings, and Mr. and Mrs. Kett carried everything out in the most lavish manner. Fortunately too, the weather, at any rate in the afternoon, left nothing to be desired. A slightly overcast sky relieved visitors from the glare and heat which have of late prevailed, and the gentle breeze rendered an outdoor function in every respect most pleasant and agreeable. Two bands were engaged for the occasion and placed on either side of the spacious lawn. The stand nearest the entrance was occupied by the Blue Hungarian Band, conducted by Mr. C. W. Clay, and the other one by the fine band of the Queen's Own Yorkshire Dragoons, under the leadership of Lieut. S. Buckley. These played alternatively so that from three o'clock until six the strains of music were constantly floating on the air and made the gathering one of the most successful ever witnessed in Cambridge. The Mayor and Mayoress received the guests just within the entrance to the gardens and extended to each a cordial and gracious welcome. Two large marquees were erected, one for teas and the other for light refreshments served from the Kitchen Department of Trinity College. We append the programmes of the two bands:--

Continued

QUEEN'S OWN YORKSHIRE DRAGOONS

Grand March ... ..."Dopple Eagle"...		Wagner
Overture ... ..."Les dieu et les Bayerdiere" ...		Auber
Concert Valse ... ..."Elsie"		Suckley
(Accepted by H.M. Majesty the Queen)		
Piccolo solo ... "Sweet Birds"		Smiths
(Soloist – Mr Vennard)		
Grand selection ... "Lohengrin"		Wagner
(Solos for the principal instruments)		
Introit ... ..."Song of the Smith" ...		Eilenberg
Valse di Concert ... ..."Blue Danube"		Strauss
Grand Selection ..."Greek Slave"...		Jones
(Solos for the principal instruments)		
Cornet solo ... "Lost Chord"		Sir A. Sullivan
(Soloist – Trumpeter J. Billam)		
Mill in the Black Forest		Michaelis
Grand Selection ... "Faust"		Gounod
(God Save the Queen)		

IMPERIAL BLUE HUNGARIAN BAND

March ... ... "Rondo des Petits Pierrots"		Bose
Caerdas ... ..."Balsoo Dal"		Misks
Morcies ... ..."Bibilage"		Gillet
Selection ... ..."Carmen"		Bizet
Mazurka ... ..."La Czarine"		Gounod
Hungarian Aire		Thiele
Walzer ... ..."Lustige Brüder"		Vollet
Caerdas ... ..."No. 1"		Michaelis
Haberano ... ... "La Paloma"		Tradler
Entracle ... ..."Vergia main nicht"		Karuly
March ... ..."Austria"		Nowotony

EVENING PARTY

The grounds were charmingly decorated for the evening party. The band stands came in for a special share of attention and there were several pretty displays in lights in different parts of the garden. A search light was also brought into use and created a considerable amount of interest. With the exception of a slight shower early in the evening, the weather was fine and the guests, who numbered over twelve hundred, thoroughly enjoyed themselves strolling about the beautiful grounds, listening to the excellent music of the two bands. The programme of the Queen's Own Yorkshire Dragoons was as under:–

Grand March	"Les Zeuvas"...	Dopler
Overture	"Raymond"	Thomas
Concert Valse	"La Jarmaine"	Waldteufel
Grand Selection ...	"Runaway Girl"	Caryll
(Soloists for the principal instruments)		
Descriptive Scene	"Sleigh Ride"	Jullies
Preparation, Start, Ride on the Road, Ball, Race, Home		
Cornet Solo	"Les Follies"	Waldteufel
(Soloist —Trumpeter Corporal J. Billam)		
Grand Selection ...	"Belle of New York"... ...	Kerker
(Soloists for the principal instruments)		
Concert Valse	"Silver Birds"	Les Thiers
(Soloist —Mr Venard)		
Euphonium Solo ...	"Selected"	
(Soloist —Mr. O. Thorn)		
Grand Selection ...	"Carmen"	Bizet
(Solos for the principal instruments)		
Descriptive Allegro ..."Jubilee Rocket"		Sackley
(Imitations of Whistling and other Rockets)		
Travestie	"Whistling Serenade"	Jones
National Selection ... 'Albion"		Baslaus
"God Save the Queen"		

The Imperial Blue Hungarian Band played the following selections:–

March	"Dorner"	Zolhrer
Waltzer	"Amour et Printempts"	Wahlteufel
Selection	"Faust"	Gounod
Ceardas	"Der Styren"	Michaelis
Entracle	"Loin du Ball"	Gillet
Ungarischen Nationalieden		Klatz

Christmas 1898

These examples of games published in the Chronicle on 23 December 1898 featuring 'charades, enigmas and puzzles', shows how anyone who had too much time on their hands over the festive season was kept amused. A notice appeared in the same paper stating that 'The Mayor recommends that all shops be closed from the Saturday evening before Christmas until the following Wednesday morning.'[14]

CHARADES

Eight letters do my whole compose,
To Jews and Christians we are foes;
The first five letters will make known
A pretty plant, and where 'tis grown;
And if you'll take the latter six,
On a famed city you will fix
Of ancient Greece, where once did dwell
Darken'd by superstitious spell,
My whole, as sacred records tell.

PUZZLES

I am a funny little thing, and there is not a day passes but what I am seen. Boys are very partial to me, and all young folks agree that they cannot do without me. I am a very useful member of society, and a staunch friend to many; and whether in prosperity or adversity, I always take the same interest in you. I am the centre of attraction in everybody, and share my favours alike with beauty and deformity. I am connected with every society and company in the world, and have shares in every railway company. I belong to the Navy, yet am equally attached to the Army, and was present with the Artillery of the Sirdar at the Battle of Omdurman. I never go to public balls or routs, but no family party would be complete without me. To give you a clue as to who I am, I can only add that without my presence it is impossible for you to be merry at the present festive season.

Answers to be found on following page.

The Mayor himself, however, was not on holiday on Christmas Day. Accompanied by Catherine and Maud Mary, he left the comfortable fireside of Wymondham House to visit the colder chambers of the Cambridge and Chesterton Workhouse. Special efforts had been made to make Christmas Day more bearable than most days for people living there. It was 'the happiest and brightest day in their whole year', insisted the *Chronicle*.

The Christmas menu at the workhouse consisted of: 'roast beef, legs of mutton, pork, sausages and plum pudding'. The Ketts stayed after dinner to talk to the residents. They distributed presents of tobacco and pipes to the men, sugar and tea to the women, and oranges and sweets to the children. Kett probably paid for the presents out of his own pocket. It must have been a stark contrast to the kind of entertainment and garden parties which he was so fond of hosting.

---

14 During Kett's last year as Mayor, most shops closed for a half day in addition to Sundays, bringing in a five and a half day week for shop staff.

Grandchildren George and Hilda in fancy dress

The menu for a dinner party at Wymondham House, 23rd June 1900. The Conservative MP Sir Penrose Fitzgerald was guest of honour, and the other guests included members of the Corporation and George Robert.

Menu

Clear Turtle
Purée of Chicken

Scotch Salmon, Lobster Sauce
Whitebait

Ris de Veau Pique aux Truffes
Chaudfroid de Mauviettes en Caises

Saddles of Lamb
Asparagus   French Beans   New Potatoes

Roast Ducklings
Green Peas

Petits savarines à la Montmorency
Chartreuse of Strawberries

Ice Pudding à la Nesselrode

Cheese Straws

DESSERT
COFFEE

FOURTEEN

THE RSPCA IN CAMBRIDGE

Animal welfare began to become an important issue in the late-nineteenth century, although animals, especially many horses, still suffered great hardship. Horses were an essential means of transport. They were often regarded as no more than instruments to be 'used up' before their lives were ended by the knacker man and they were converted into dog meat. Many a Newmarket racehorse ended up between the shafts of a Hansom Cab, and furious driving caused many accidents, often fatal for both horses and humans. The newspapers were always full of such incidents.

An outbreak of 'Glanders' (an infectious and fatal equine disease hardly ever seen today) in Cambridge in 1899 caused great concern, although to some owners the concern was purely financial. The Kett family kept many horses for business and personal use, but to George Kett they were not merely machines. He and his family showed an affection for their animals, and Kett was pleased to chair a meeting for the Cambridge branch of the RSPCA in the summer of 1899. His speech on this occasion was unusually full of personal concern and reminiscences about animals.

'Those of us', he began, 'who can look back on 40 or 50 years in Cambridge will vividly appreciate the difference between the conditions of the horses and dogs in our streets now and then. It was quite a common sight 40 or 50 years ago to see a poor decrepit old horse covered with an old sack for the purposes of shielding the eyes of the public from the deplorable state the animal was in. With regard to dogs, I am old enough to remember that it was a common thing to see from one to five or six dogs harnessed to a load of crockery, or some other such commodity, which was being hawked about the street from place to place. More than once I have seen a dog drop dead from over-exertion. They were urged on with whips, and sights were seen such as one could hardly understand nowadays, but no official notice seemed to have been taken in those times. Since then, we are glad to know that many Acts of Parliament have been passed with a view to bettering the conditions of animals and very much has been done by the RSPCA to enforce those Acts and do away with a great amount of misery which the animals had hitherto experienced.'

Kett continued with obvious concern. 'It is sad to think,' he said, 'that although the Society has been established for over three-quarters of a century, the cases which it searches out do not diminish but, according to the report, continually increase. According to the statement I have seen of 1897, no fewer than 7,545 convictions were obtained at the police courts through the instrumentality of the Society; which shows a terrible amount of suffering and ill-usage inflicted upon animals by certain classes. Of course, a few years previous to that which I referred to, it was common practice to barbarously ill-treat and mutilate horses in a way that in the present time would not be permitted. I allude to the custom of clipping horses ears and cutting their tails in order to make them curve. And these were not poor men's horses, but the hunters and hacks of the wealthy. I believe a regiment of cavalry treated all their horses in the same way.'

Grandson George

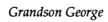

George Robert

Kett returned to the issue of local anti-animal cruelty towards the end of his speech. 'The Cambridge branch of the Society has been established for 20 years, and has done good work in the neighbourhood. I was asked this morning a question I could not answer, viz, where was the office of the local branch and where could the officer be found? The gentleman who asked me the question assured me also that if the Committee could see their way to add to their numbers by including a number of gentlemen in the immediate neighbourhood it would be of great service to the Society and would considerably augment the funds. The gentleman in question volunteered to give £25 a year for a time until everything was established, and more if it was needed. He was sure that other friends would likewise assist to any reasonable extent.' Here the audience applauded their approval, so Kett continued, 'I would like to ask the Committee whether they thought it was worthwhile to take such suggestions into consideration. People in the country have opportunity of seeing and hearing of cases of cruelty which perhaps we in the towns do not often meet with. If anything resulted from the suggestion I am sure that it would give great satisfaction to many who are anxious to assist in the work of preventing cruelty to animals, and it would also help the Society to carry on its work more perfectly than it had as yet been able to do.'

There was a storm of applause. Much-needed publicity and funds were raised for the local branch of the RSPCA. The Master of Trinity College warmly thanked the Mayor. 'I would like to thank the Mayor, not only for taking the Chair and giving the whole weight of his personal influence to the cause, but also for the emphatic way in which he had expressed sympathy with the Society and the wise council he has tendered us.'

Kett's second year as Mayor ended with tributes and celebrations in November 1899. Thirteen months later the nineteenth century came to an end.

The mayor's carriage

FIFTEEN

A CANCELLED CELEBRATION

Queen Victoria's long reign, begun the year after Kett's birth, ended with her death in 1901. The turn of the twentieth century heralded a new monarch, King Edward VII, who was almost sixty. His Coronation ceremony was planned for 26 June 1902, after the mourning period for Queen Victoria had ended. For town councils all over the country, 1902 was set to be an exceptionally busy year. The celebrations for the Coronation were organised on as grand a scale as each town could possibly manage (there was no little pride attached to this); and in addition there were the usual tasks of local government.

After a year's break, Kett was again elected Mayor in November 1901. It was to be his third and final term of office. It was also his most important year as Mayor. He was especially proud of the honour of presiding over Cambridge's celebrations of King Edward's Coronation, but no-one could have predicted the difficulties which lay ahead.

Kett's five-year term of office as Alderman also ended in November 1901, when voting took place for the election or re-election of Aldermen. Twenty-nine members of the Council voted for Kett (more than for any other Alderman), and Kett agreed to serve for a further five years.

Throughout that winter, thoughts continually turned to the summer. The festivities planned in Cambridge were set to surpass even the grand Jubilee celebrations of five summers before.

For Kett, the Coronation day promised to be a memorable one. As Chief Magistrate of Cambridge he was invited to Westminster Abbey for the ceremony. Months before the day dawned, plans were made by special committees for all of Cambridge to spend the national holiday in style. The summer of 1902 produced superb weather, which facilitated the work which went into the preparation. A few days before the event everything was ready. Bunting, fairy lights and flags lined every street, and small gold crowns decorated the lamp posts. The Corporation decided (with the approval of the King) that instead of spending ten guineas on an 'illuminated address' to send to the Palace, the money should be donated instead to the King's Hospital Fund. A plain address of congratulations was sent instead, signed by George Kett, as Mayor on 21 June 1902.

Suddenly, a few days before the ceremony was due to take place, the elderly King fell ill, suffering from appendicitis. He seemed to recover a little but then relapsed so that an operation was necessary. The King was extremely ill and it was thought that he might possibly die. It became obvious that the ceremony would have to be indefinitely postponed. Although the celebrations in London were cancelled, the King sent notice that events in provincial places should go ahead as planned.

Kett immediately called an emergency meeting of the Chairmen of the local Coronation Committees. Everything was thrown into confusion. Apparently the lack of official notification from the Palace made it difficult to determine what to do at the eleventh hour. The Town Clerk pointed out that the King had wished the celebrations to go ahead

Coronation Notice to Guests

in the towns. However, since there was considerable doubt that the King would survive his illness and the operation, the majority of the Committee Chairmen, including Kett, thought it unthinkable to go ahead in the circumstances.

Workmen were sent out immediately to remove the flags, bunting and lamps, yet somehow they forgot to take down the crowns, which continued to glitter hopelessly in the June sunshine. A whole host of supplies had to be dealt with. There were large quantities of meat, cakes, and other provisions already on their way. One of the

CORONATION
OF KING EDWARD VII.
JUNE 26th, 1902.

Borough of Cambridge
Coronation Festivities.

ALDERMAN GEORGE KETT, J.P., MAYOR.

DINNER TO 2,500 OLD PEOPLE.

On PARKER'S PIECE.

Bill of Fare.

ROAST BEEF.	ROAST LAMB AND MINT SAUCE.	
BOILED BEEF.	PRESSED BEEF.	YORK HAM.
GALANTINE OF VEAL.	RAISED PIES.	

DRESSED SALADS.   PICKLES.   ROLLS.

STEWED FRUITS.   CUSTARDS.   FRUIT JELLIES.
FRUIT TARTS.

CHEESE.   BUTTER.   BISCUITS.

GINGER BEER.   ALE.   LEMONADE.

Owing to the illness of His Majesty the King, the dinner was postponed and the food provided was given away at the Corn Exchange. On Thursday, September 4th, 1902, in conjunction with a tea to 6,000 school children, the dinner as above was given to those inhabitants of the town (about 250) who were present at the Cambridge festivities in connection with the coronation of Her Late Majesty Queen Victoria, in 1838.

Councillors wanted to cancel the meat order, but the animals had already been killed and it would have been unfair on the butcher to turn down such a huge order. The food had to be received as agreed.

Finally it was decided that the food would be given away at the Corn Exchange. Kett announced with obvious disappointment that the Children's Tea planned for 6,000 youngsters and the dinner for 2,500 old people were also postponed. A glance at the bill of fare on the previous page indicates the quantity and cost of food involved.

It must have been disappointing for everyone, and a particularly trying time for the Mayor. Later the same day printed bills were circulated in the town with the message: 'Owing to the serious illness of His Majesty the King, I recommend that all coronation festivities be postponed indefinitely. George Kett. Guildhall. 24th June 1902.'

Crowds gathered that evening around Market Hill to read the telegraphs giving the latest news which were posted outside the newspaper offices. Some, who had been looking forward to the holiday and the festivities, were disappointed by the Committee's decision to postpone events. Most thought, though, that it would have been wrong to indulge in rejoicing while the King was so ill and might possibly die. A notice was posted to the effect that the King had died, but this was quickly followed by a wire which stated that the King had had the operation and was as well as could be expected. Everything was thrown into chaos and for a while no-one knew quite what to believe. Eventually everyone reluctantly realised that there was no hope of the festivities going ahead, and lingered around before going home. For a while the King's prospects of recovery looked bleak, but he gradually began to recover, and the following month he was out of danger.

At the next meeting of the Town Council in July, Councillor Digby criticised Kett's decision to call an emergency meeting exclusively made up of Chairmen and Secretaries of the Committees. He thought that the whole Council should have been called together, and challenged the Mayor to defend his decision. Undaunted, Kett replied, 'I think I took the proper course, as things were all in working order and the only matter requiring consideration was the question of what to do with the provisions.' Alderman Peck disagreed, and said so; 'In my opinion, there should have been a meeting of the whole Council first.' Kett replied by addressing the original complainant, Digby. 'I believe that a meeting of the whole Council was unnecessary, and I acted as I thought fit. Do you propose to alter the formation of the various committees?' he asked. 'Not at all', came the reply, and after several Councillors spoke in support of Kett, his decision was accepted.

Kett was quite decided that a weak or easily-influenced Mayor could not be a successful one. As he explained in a later speech, 'I do not think you should listen to every opinion that is offered, because I think the less you do so the better. Once having asked you are bound to a certain extent to carry out a friend's suggestion, while at the same time there's another equally good friend who thinks the contrary way. I think the best thing is to use all the common sense and discretion you can, and then people will give you credit for doing your best.'

Nevertheless, the whole occasion was disappointing and expensive. The illness of King Edward which prevented his coronation in June 1902, and the accompanying mayhem, has now been almost completely forgotten.

SIXTEEN

A CORONATION CEREMONY

The King recovered remarkably quickly, and plans were made for his Coronation early in September. Nearly 70 Council meetings had been called to make the original arrangements and a further 20 were squeezed into July and August. This time everything went exactly as arranged. The only disappointment was the weather, the bright June sunshine was merely a memory as a grey autumn day dawned for the coronation.

Kett missed the Cambridge celebrations, for he was at Westminster, surrounded by the most important and influential people in the country who were crowded into Westminster Abbey. It was an occasion Kett was never to forget.

In Cambridge, the celebrations were in full-swing, with fireworks, carriage competitions, races, concerts, and a balloon ascent. Great crowds of people wallowed in an atmosphere of excitement. Every house was decorated including, needless to say, Wymondham House, which was dressed up in bunting for the day. The house formed a centre-piece for a collage of photographs taken by Edmund Kett to commemorate the occasion. Like the Jubilee festivities, the Coronation celebrations carried on throughout the week, and on his return Kett was able to enjoy the fun.

Wanderers Cycling Club car, coronation procession. Cambridgeshire Collection.

FROM THE CAMBRIDGE DAILY NEWS CORONATION SOUVENIR SEPTEMBER 1902

The procession

One of the cars

ON CHRIST'S PIECES.

'On Christ's Pieces', from the Cambridge Daily News Coronation Souvenir, September 1902

The Coronation Tea and Dinner for children and old people was held on Parker's Piece. All the Kett family joined in to help. George Robert waited at table during the celebration dinner held for the old people. George Kett had a splendid time, reported the Chronicle. 'The Mayor must hold a high place in the affections of thousands of the juveniles of Cambridge. It is astonishing how quickly Alderman Kett won the favour of the children entertained on Parker's Piece. With his beaming countenance, scarlet gown, and cocked hat, he was always the centre of attraction, and after tea, when he had distributed many of the coronation medals, he was followed by a small crowd of admiring boys and girls.'

On the Friday, the Mayor and Mayoress visited 16 schools to distribute medals. 'In one school,' reported the Chronicle, 'it was a little amusing to hear the piping voices of the infants in rollicking song, "For he's a jolly good fellow", directly his Worship put in an appearance.' These were Kett's most brilliant days.

A few months after the Coronation celebrations were over, the Mayoral year came to an end. Kett handed over the Chain of Office for the last time. In November 1902 he accepted the role of Deputy Mayor, continuing his work within the Committees.

Kett undoubtedly spent vast amounts of his personal fortune during his years in office. This hospitality, coupled with his enthusiasm for work, had made him an ideal Mayor. It was time for the community to repay Kett – not financially, but by their appreciation.

The Corporation and town went out of their way to honour the ageing man. There were many complimentary speeches in his honour. Among the speakers was Dr Alex Hill, Master of Downing College. He said, 'When I look at Mr Kett it always comes to mind that he is emphatically good. His dinners are good – they might be expensive, but that is his affair! His work is good. I have heard people say that it is expensive, but that is simply due to a confusion of ideas, for although you may get an appearance of finish and solidity for a little money it is never in the end the cheapest at any price – and anyone who knows Mr Kett would say that his heart is good.' Here Dr Hill stopped for the loud applause. 'Here the money element does not come into it, its price is above rubies. Of all those who have served the town in the high office which Alderman Kett has recently held, no-one had been more willing and more ready to give his fellow citizens his very best.'

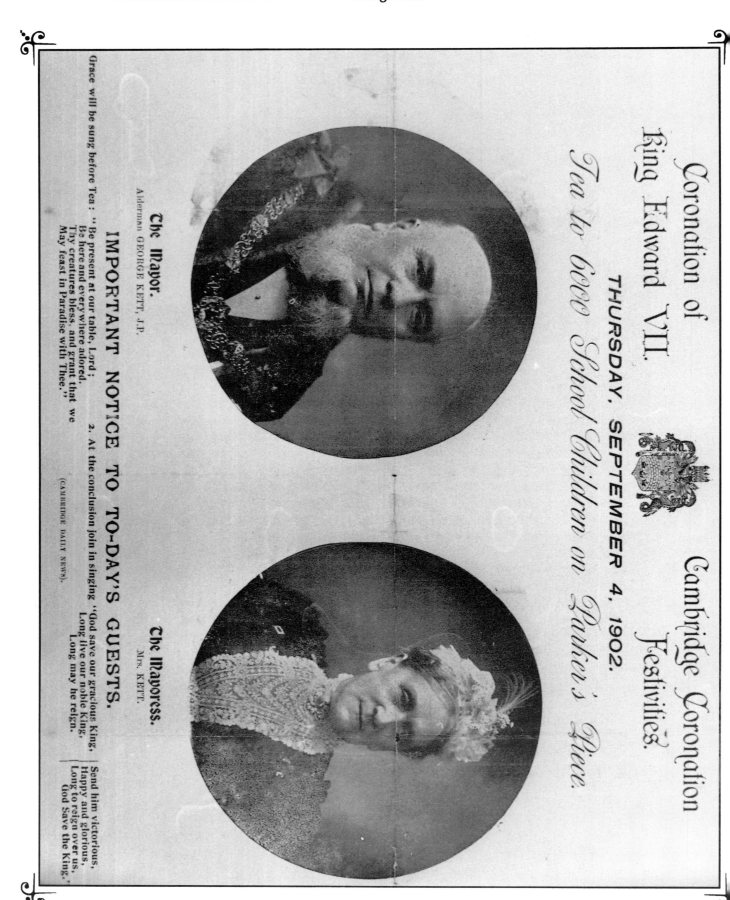

Details of the childrens tea party reproduced from Cambridge Daily News.

SEVENTEEN

A PRESENTATION

K ett's attendance level at Council meetings were always amongst the highest of the members, even in the years when he was not Mayor. For example, during the years 1899 to 1900 – the break between his last two Mayoral years – he served on the following committees:

Assessment Committee
Guildhall and Building Committee
Watch Committee
Parliamentary Committee
Sewage Disposal Committee
Special Committee regarding extra accommodation for the Police.

During his second year of Mayoralty Kett attended all 18 Council meetings, and was one of only three Councillors to manage this. On one occasion when he was Mayor he was unable to attend a Quarterly Meeting due to illness. He had fallen ill through working an over-long shift on the Magisterial Bench and then going on to a prize presentation he had promised to attend. This had resulted in his being confined to bed for a week.

However much George Kett loved to work, the years were beginning to catch up with him. He was 67 in 1903, and it was obvious that the days of Kett's Mayoralty were over forever. A Kett Testimonial Committee, headed by the new Mayor, was set up, and over 300 people subscribed to it in order to raise funds for a suitable gift. Although the Committee was initially kept secret, it was decided in the end to ask Kett what he would like to receive. He chose to have a portrait of himself painted by C E Brook.

Both Catherine and Maud Mary were invited to accompany Kett to the presentation evening – Maud Mary because she had held the office of Mayoress in 1891–2 and had then assisted her father and mother with municipal duties over the years. Yet she was ill with a 'chill' on the day of the presentation, and was unable to personally receive the diamond and gold pendant presented to her in acknowledgement of her duties. Catherine received a diamond and sapphire brooch, and George a gold repeater watch and a large silver tray.

The Guildhall on the Monday of the presentation in May 1903 was packed with Kett's friends and colleagues. The new Mayor, Councillor P H Young, focused on the main events of Kett's Mayoral years. At the mention that Kett had served for 21 years on the Council, a storm of applause erupted. The new Mayor ended by assuring the audience that Kett was not leaving the Council. 'I trust', he ended, 'we shall have the benefit of Alderman Kett's sage advice and experience, for many years to come.'

The Vice-Chancellor of the University spoke after the Mayor, saying, 'Alderman Kett has given to his friends and fellow townsmen of his best, and his best has been very good.'

During his speech of thanks, Kett indicated his debt to his own family. 'I am pleased to have the opportunity of expressing in public my gratitude for the great assistance I receive from my own household. It is well known that I am engaged in a business of my own, and only through the great assistance rendered me by my two sons was I able to devote my time to the services of the town. With regard to social duties, my wife and daughter are always ready to help in any scheme considered for the amusement of our friends, and I am much indebted to them.' He finished by thanking everyone again, saying that he hoped 'The longer I live, the more friends I will make.'

EIGHTEEN

THE REMAINING YEARS

Active hard-working people usually retain these characteristics as long as their health allows. Although Kett jokingly referred to the Chain of Office as a 'burden', there was no doubt that he loved public life and gave it up only when his health began to deteriorate. Eventually George Kett retired from business in 1904 and allowed George Robert and Edmund to take control. He continued to work in his capacity as Alderman until 1913. Elected Director of the Cambridge Water Company in 1900, he served the Water Board[15] until his death.

Kett was able to devote more time to his research into family history during his last years. It is easy to imagine Kett as an old man sitting at his desk in Wymondham House sorting though masses of old documents. The amount of research he achieved is phenomenal. The following generations of Ketts must have inherited his love of genealogy since the family tree he drew up has been kept up-to-date.

On 5 August 1907, Catherine died at home. She had suffered from progressive muscular atrophy for over two years. She was buried in the Kett plot at Mill Road Cemetery, next to the grave of her eldest daughter.

During the years after his wife's death, Kett's health began to fail and a nurse, Jessie Skates, was employed to look after him. Maud Mary kept her father company and was helped by servants Ethel, Jessie and Emmeline. The garden was tended by a full- time gardener, Cole, with the coachman Chapman making up the full complement of the staff at Wymondham House.

Kett's friends and colleagues did not forget him during this time, and in 1913 another presentation was made to him by the Council.

With the help of a relation by marriage, Mr Campling, the great Kett 'pedigree' was prepared for publication, and finally published in 1913 bound in hard-back and on quality paper. Presentation copies were made to all Kett's children, and to the Cambridge Free Library. Ironically, by this time Kett's eyesight had completely failed, and he was, 'never able to read the pages his loving and life-long efforts had done so much to prepare.' He could move about now only in his invalid chair, although his mental faculties were not impaired.

In March, 1914, George Kett became so weak that he was no longer able to leave Wymondham House. He died at home of heart failure, on 6 Mary 1914, aged 77.

---

15 In 1903 cases of typhoid fever occurred at the Fulbourn Asylum and the risk of pollution of the Fulbourn well from the rather primitive sewage disposal works of the Asylum, although remote, could not be excluded. The Water Board decided to seek statutory powers to sterilise water by treatment with chlorine or ozone. This is believed to be the first such undertaking by a water company in the United Kingdom, but consent was refused by the House of Lords Committee. (From 'Cambridge Water Company – A Brief History', compiled by G A Moores and published by the Cambridge Water Company.)

The preface of Kett's family history, with his personal view of his ancestor Robert Kett, is reproduced below.

THE KETT PEDIGREE

The family of Kett, of Wymondham, in the County of Norfolk, was established there at least as early as the twelfth century, and has continued in Wymondham in unbroken line, to the present day. Their history shows unusual vicissitudes of fortune; for more than 300 years (1200–1550) they advanced in wealth and position, until the family attained and appeared likely to retain, a prominent and permanent place among the gentlefolk of the County. The sudden tragedy of the failure of the Rebellion in East Anglia, in 1549, conceived and headed in the masterful personality of ROBERT KETT, stayed the hitherto steady advance of the family; and for generations the attainer and execution of the leaders was severely visited on their descendants.

The shadow of the failure of the insurrection gradually passed away, and the Ketts became numerous and wide-spread, and rose again to position in Norfolk. A branch left the country and took some part in the earlier development of our West Indian Colonies; returning to settle in Suffolk in the eighteenth century. The following pages sum up the many references to the family in the national and local archives, and present a concise record of the ancestry, connections and descendants of Robert Kett.

History has pronounced this judgement on him: that he was a man in advance of his time – a man who staked his life in the struggle against the wrongs of this fellow-countrymen.

The prayers of his noble petition to King Edward VI, were not offered up in vain; and the liberties he sought, unattainable in his day, have now become the guarantees of a freedom from oppression, envied – it is not too much to say – by every other nation in the civilised world. "We pray thatt all bonde men can be made ffre, for God made all ffre with his precious blode sheddyng."

This forerunner of Rousseau, followed the teaching of his Master in giving up his life for the people whom God had made free, but who were yet found everywhere in chains.

The history of the man Robert Kett is, in a measure, the history of our nation; a somewhat blind groping towards freedom, by means that show singleness and honesty of purpose, yet which are faulty in themselves. It will be seen that others of Robert Kett's blood have not hesitated in their turn to offer their lives in the conviction of the justness of their cause; and so to pass on the tradition to their children.

Descendants of those men have compiled this record of an English family, with its complement of great and worthy men, in the confidence that they who shall follow may ever keep in mind the unselfish aims and achievements of men of their name and blood, long since dead, but not forgotten.

I should like to place on record the great assistance rendered to me in the preparation of these tables by the late Mr EB Pomeroy, of Wymondham, and by Mr Arthur Campling, and my gratitude to Miss Marion Kett for abstracting the Manorial Court Rolls of Forncett, and many other documents.

George Kett

4 June 1913

George and Catherine's grave next to Catherine Sarah's which has unfortunately been badly broken. Mill Road Cemetery, Cambridge

Unveiling the 'Lone Soldier', Station Road Corner. Grandson George in his uniform lifts his hat (immediately to the left of King George V).

NINETEEN

THE NEXT GENERATION

The Kett family continued to be prominent in Cambridge after George Kett's death. George Robert and Edmund managed Rattee and Kett after their father's death. During the First World War, George Robert was made the executive officer for food control in Cambridge and District, and was awarded an OBE for his services in 1920. He became President of the Master Builders Association and was a Fellow of the Institute of Builders (George Kett had been Vice-President).

Edmund retired in 1926, and the company was sold to the Mowlem group in that year. The name Rattee and Kett was retained, and George Robert continued as Chairman until just before his death in 1933. George Robert's son George was a Captain during the Second World War and travelled extensively. He was widowed twice before marrying Edith Mary Jones. They had one child, a daughter called Mary, in 1949. Grandson George spent his later years in Cambridge, living at 18 Station Road until it was demolished, and then moving to 6 Claremont, Hills Road. He died in 1970.

Like many other Cambridge people, Kett's great-granddaughter Mary, remembers walking past the Station Road offices of Rattee and Kett which were destroyed to make way for a new concrete office block in 1960. Appropriately, the office block is called 'Kett House', and the decoration on the front of the building is a modern sculpture representing rebel-farmer Robert Kett holding a meeting with the rebels and featuring 'Kett's Oak'. The Rattee and Kett's Purbeck Road site remains standing today.

KETT HOUSE

The destruction of Rattee and Kett's Station Road premises. The new office block can be seen in the background.

One of the first Rattee & Kett motorised vehicles

EPILOGUE

WYMONDHAM HOUSE

'All houses wherein men have lived and died are haunted houses.'
Longfellow

After her father's death[16], Maud Mary remained at Wymondham House for ten years, finally leaving in 1924. Maud Mary then lived at 18 Station Road, the house once occupied by her Grandfather, although in her later years she travelled a great deal. During the last years of her life, her nephew George and his wife lived with her at No. 18. She remained a strict Victorian Aunt, occupying the best rooms in the house while George and his wife had to make do with the top and bottom storeys.

In 1924 Wymondham House was sold to the Reverend P R Allnutt for £5,500. Only the house and two plots bought in 1879 were sold, the other small adjoining plot remaining in the Kett family at that time. The Rev Allnutt left the property to a relative, spinster Alice Lea Deardean, on 21 May 1930. She sold it six months later, to Mabel Simpson, for £2,500.

Around this time the house was divided into flatlets, although not many structural alterations were made. Mabel and her sister Ethel Warren-Wilson lived in the best rooms on the ground-floor. Ethel's granddaughters Anne and Frances remember staying at Wymondham House during the 1950s, when it was 'Very cold and quite dark'. In spite of this, both remember the house with affection. When Anne was engaged to be married, her Grandmother promised her the carved wooden doors and the wrought-iron garden gate! Thankfully they remained in their proper place. However, the strip of land at the back of the garden beyond the garden gate where the Kett horses had once been stabled was given away in 1951, in payment of a debt.

Mabel died in 1961 in the Hope Nursing Home opposite the house, and left the property to her niece and her husband John Francis Richard Ince. He continued to let the property to students, although the underground rooms were declared unfit for human habitation in 1968.

Mr Ince applied for permission for change of use of the property to offices. This was refused in 1971. Ince appealed against the decision, saying 'The residential allocation on the plan is outdated and irrelevant, the character of Brooklands Avenue having changed over recent years. The present house is ugly, too large as a single family unit by present day standards, and not easily divisible into flatlets.'

Fortunately, the appeal was turned down. In June 1973 the property was sold to the Bank of Europe Limited for £43,000. When the site was inspected in April 1974, Kett's former home was described as 'a large vacant house'.

After three applications for the change of use of the house and property had been

---

16 All the female servants in Kett's employment received a year's wages, and all the men servants half a year's pay, as instructed in Kett's Will.

turned down, Wymondham House was sold to Mr and Mrs G P Reece on 13 May 1975 for £39,000.

The National Extension College (NEC), looking for a new home after moving from 131 Hills Road, inspected the house and applied for change of use in 1977. At last, permission was granted, and NEC bought the property in September 1978.

NEC's Director, Ros Morpeth, is committed to preserving the character of the house.

Bibliography

'Who's Who in Norfolk, Suffolk and Cambridgeshire 1912'
Published by H Cox 'Field' Office, Windsor House, London.

'Cambridgeshire and Huntingdonshire Leaders'
By Ernest Gaskell. Published by The Queenhithe Printing and Publishing Co Ltd, 13 Bread Street Hill, Queen Victoria Street, London EC

'Victorian Cambridge'
by Glynn Thomas. Published by Dobson Books Ltd, 80 Kensington Church Street, London W8

'Later Victorian Cambridge'
By D A Winstanley, published by Cambridge University Press, Shaftesbury Road, Cambridge

'Town and Gown'
By Rowland Parker, published by Patrick Stephens Limited, Bar Hill, Cambridge.

'Cambridge Guide (1845)'.
Published by Metcalfe & Palmer, Trinity Street, Cambridge.

'East Anglian Studies'
Edited by Lionel M Menby, published by W Heffer & Sons Ltd, Cambridge.

'The East Anglians'
By Ronald Fletcher, published by Patrick Stephens Limited, Bar Hill, Cambridge.

'The Pedigree of Kett of Wymondham Co Norfolk AD 1180–1913'
By George Kett. Privately published in Cambridge.

Kelly's Directory of Cambridge
Spaldings Directory of Cambridge

Cambridge City Council Minutes
1891–92, 1898–99, 1901–02

Cambridge Independent Press
Cambridge Graphic
Cambridge Chronicle and University Journal
Cambridge Daily News
Cambridge Evening News and Weekly News Series